WITHDRAWN

GERONIMO

NORTH AMERICAN INDIANS OF ACHIEVEMENT

GERONIMO
Apache Warrior

▼▼▼

Melissa Schwarz

Senior Consulting Editor
W. David Baird
Howard A. White Professor of History
Pepperdine University

CHELSEA HOUSE PUBLISHERS

New York   Philadelphia

FRONTISPIECE The earliest known picture of Geronimo, taken by A. Frank Randall in the spring of 1884.

ON THE COVER An original painting from a photograph of Geronimo taken in 1886 by Camillus Fly.

Chelsea House Publishers
EDITOR-IN-CHIEF Remmel Nunn
MANAGING EDITOR Karyn Gullen Browne
COPY CHIEF Mark Rifkin
PICTURE EDITOR Adrian G. Allen
ART DIRECTOR Maria Epes
ASSISTANT ART DIRECTOR Noreen Romano
MANUFACTURING DIRECTOR Gerald Levine
SYSTEMS MANAGER Lindsey Ottman
PRODUCTION MANAGER Joseph Romano
PRODUCTION COORDINATOR Marie Claire Cebrián

North American Indians of Achievement
SENIOR EDITOR Liz Sonneborn

Staff for *GERONIMO*
ASSISTANT EDITOR Brian Sookram
COPY EDITOR Benson D. Simmonds
EDITORIAL ASSISTANT Michele Haddad
DESIGNER Debora Smith
PICTURE RESEARCHER Vicky Haluska
COVER ILLUSTRATION Vilma Ortiz

First Printing

1 3 5 7 9 8 6 4 2

Library of Congress Cataloging-in-Publication Data

Schwarz, Melissa.
Geronimo/Melissa Schwarz.
p. cm.—(North American Indians of Achievement)
Summary: Examines the life and career of the Apache warrior chief.
ISBN 0-7910-1701-X
1. Geronimo, Apache Chief, 1829–1909. 2. Apache Indians—Biography. 3. Apache Indians—Wars. [1. Geronimo, Apache Chief, 1829–1909. 2. Apache Indians—Biography. 3. Indians of North America—Southwest, New—Biography.] I. Title. II. Series.
E99.A6G3273 1991   91-12691
979'.00497—dc20   CIP
[B]   AC

CONTENTS

NORTH AMERICAN INDIANS OF ACHIEVEMENT

BLACK HAWK
Sac Rebel

JOSEPH BRANT
Mohawk Chief

COCHISE
Apache Chief

CRAZY HORSE
Sioux War Chief

CHIEF GALL
Sioux War Chief

GERONIMO
Apache Warrior

HIAWATHA
Founder of the Iroquois
Confederacy

CHIEF JOSEPH
Nez Percé Leader

PETER MACDONALD
Former Chairman of the Navajo
Nation

WILMA MANKILLER
Principal Chief of the Cherokees

OSCEOLO
Seminole Rebel

QUANAH PARKER
Comanche Chief

KING PHILIP
Wampanoag Rebel

**POCAHONTAS AND CHIEF
POWHATAN**
Leaders of the Powhatan Tribes

PONTIAC
Ottawa Rebel

RED CLOUD
Sioux War Chief

WILL ROGERS
Cherokee Entertainer

SEQUOYAH
Inventor of the Cherokee Alphabet

SITTING BULL
Chief of the Sioux

TECUMSEH
Shawnee Rebel

JIM THORPE
Sac and Fox Athlete

SARAH WINNEMUCCA
Northern Paiute Writer and
Diplomat

Other titles in preparation

ON INDIAN LEADERSHIP

by W. David Baird
Howard A. White Professor of History
Pepperdine University

Authoritative utterance is in thy mouth, perception is in thy heart, and thy tongue is the shrine of justice," the ancient Egyptians said of their king. From him, the Egyptians expected authority, discretion, and just behavior. Homer's *Iliad* suggests that the Greeks demanded somewhat different qualities from their leaders: justice and judgment, wisdom and counsel, shrewdness and cunning, valor and action. It is not surprising that different people living at different times should seek different qualities from the individuals they looked to for guidance. By and large, a people's requirements for leadership are determined by two factors: their culture and the unique circumstances of the time and place in which they live.

Before the late 15th century, when non-Indians first journeyed to what is now North America, most Indian tribes were not ruled by a single person. Instead, there were village chiefs, clan headmen, peace chiefs, war chiefs, and a host of other types of leaders, each with his or her own specific duties. These influential people not only decided political matters but also helped shape their tribe's social, cultural, and religious life. Usually, Indian leaders held their positions because they had won the respect of their peers. Indeed, if a leader's followers at any time decided that he or she was out of step with the will of the people, they felt free to look to someone else for advice and direction.

Thus, the greatest achievers in traditional Indian communities were men and women of extraordinary talent. They were not only skilled at navigating the deadly waters of tribal politics and cultural customs but also able to, directly or indirectly, make a positive and significant difference in the daily life of their followers.

From the beginning of their interaction with Native Americans, non-Indians failed to understand these features of Indian leadership. Early European explorers and settlers merely assumed that Indians had the same relationship with their leaders as non-Indians had with their kings and queens. European monarchs generally inherited their positions and ruled large nations however they chose, often with little regard for the desires or needs of their subjects. As a result, the settlers of Jamestown saw Pocahontas as a "princess" and Pilgrims dubbed Wampanoag leader Metacom "King Philip," envisioning them in roles very different from those in which their own people placed them.

As more and more non-Indians flocked to North America, the nature of Indian leadership gradually began to change. Influential Indians no longer had to take on the often considerable burden of pleasing only their own people; they also had to develop a strategy of dealing with the non-Indian newcomers. In a rapidly changing world, new types of Indian role models with new ideas and talents continually emerged. Some were warriors; others were peacemakers. Some held political positions within their tribes; others were writers, artists, religious prophets, or athletes. Although the demands of Indian leadership altered from generation to generation, several factors that determined which Indian people became prominent in the centuries after first contact remained the same.

Certain personal characteristics distinguished these Indians of achievement. They were intelligent, imaginative, practical, daring, shrewd, uncompromising, ruthless, and logical. They were constant in friendships, unrelenting in hatreds, affectionate with their relatives, and respectful to their God or gods. Of course, no single Native American leader embodied all these qualities, nor these qualities only. But it was these characteristics that allowed them to succeed.

The special skills and talents that certain Indians possessed also brought them to positions of importance. The life of Hiawatha, the legendary founder of the powerful Iroquois Confederacy, displays the value that oratorical ability had for many Indians in power.

The biography of Cochise, the 19th-century Apache chief, illustrates that leadership often required keen diplomatic skills not only in transactions among tribespeople but also in hardheaded negotiations with non-Indians. For others, such as Mohawk Joseph Brant and Navajo Peter MacDonald, a non-Indian education proved advantageous in their dealings with other peoples.

Sudden changes in circumstance were another crucial factor in determining who became influential in Indian communities. King Philip in the 1670s and Geronimo in the 1880s both came to power when their people were searching for someone to lead them into battle against white frontiersmen who had forced upon them a long series of indignities. Seeing the rising discontent of Indians of many tribes in the 1810s, Tecumseh and his brother, the Shawnee prophet Tenskwatawa, proclaimed a message of cultural revitalization that appealed to thousands. Other Indian achievers recognized cooperation with non-Indians as the most advantageous path during their lifetime. Sarah Winnemucca in the late 19th century bridged the gap of understanding between her people and their non-Indian neighbors through the publication of her autobiography *Life Among the Piutes*. Olympian Jim Thorpe in the early 20th century championed the assimilationist policies of the U.S. government and, with his own successes, demonstrated the accomplishments Indians could make in the non-Indian world. And Wilma Mankiller, principal chief of the Cherokees, continues to fight successfully for the rights of her people through the courts and through negotiation with federal officials.

Leadership among Native Americans, just as among all other peoples, can be understood only in the context of culture and history. But the centuries that Indians have had to cope with invasions of foreigners in their homelands have brought unique hardships and obstacles to the Native American individuals who most influenced and inspired others. Despite these challenges, there has never been a lack of Indian men and women equal to these tasks. With such strong leaders, it is no wonder that Native Americans remain such a vital part of this nation's cultural landscape.

*Ruins of an ancient city
at Casas Grandes, in the
Mexican state of Chihuahua.
The Chihuahuan authorities
negotiated a temporary peace
with the Apaches in 1849,
after many years of war
between the two peoples.*

1

APACHE REVENGE

Deep in the Gila Mountains, in what is now Arizona, a young Apache joined his fellow warriors as they departed their camp on a cool night in 1850. Guided by the stars, the Indians moved quickly on foot over the rocky cliffs and flat, arid valleys of their homeland. They were heading south to trade goods in Chihuahua, one of two Mexican states bordering their territory. The Apache warrior, who would come to be known as Geronimo, was accompanied by his wife, widowed mother, and two small children. In a cradleboard carried on his wife's back, a baby rode comfortably. It would be a long trip, but not a difficult one. Geronimo and his family had made the journey regularly since the previous summer when the Apaches, under chief Mangas Coloradas (Spanish for Red Sleeves), negotiated a peace treaty with Chihuahua.

On their way to the Mexican town of Casas Grandes, where they were expected, the Indians decided to pitch camp near a river outside Janos, a town in northern Chihuahua. As the women set up camp, the men gathered together the items for trade—cured animal hides and furs, wild herbs, and goods that they had acquired during raids in the neighboring Mexican state of Sonora. In return, they expected to receive knives, brightly colored cloth, beads, and mescal, a popular alcoholic drink.

11

Sometimes the authorities in Casas Grandes gave them food rations as well to ensure that peace would continue. The governor of Chihuahua considered it a small price to pay, for the Apaches were most formidable as enemies.

At the river encampment, Geronimo said good-bye to his family and left with the other warriors to go into Janos. Because they were enjoying a rare period of good relations with the Mexicans of Chihuahua, the warriors took minimum precautions, leaving behind only two men to guard the women and children. War with the Mexicans had been a part of Apache life for so long that most of these Indians believed that the two peoples had always been enemies. Since the arrival of Spanish conquistadores on Apache land in the 1590s, the Apaches had made hundreds of raids, and hundreds of people on both sides had been killed in battle.

As Geronimo and the other warriors were returning to camp, relaxed and happy from a profitable day of trading

Apache warriors on a night raid. In Apache philosophy, the purpose of war was to kill enemies, but raids were undertaken to steal property.

at Janos, they were met by a small group of their women and children with the news that Mexican troops from Sonora had attacked the river encampment. They had killed the guards, taken ponies and supplies, and massacred many people. The remaining Apaches quickly dispersed and found hiding places in the hills. They agreed to meet after nightfall at a prearranged place. Many years later, Geronimo recalled in his memoirs the scene that night:

> Silently we stole in one by one: sentinels were placed, and, when all were counted, I found that my aged mother, my young wife, and my three small children were among the slain. . . . Without being noticed I silently turned away and stood by the river, how long I stood there, I do not know. It was decided that as there were only eighty warriors left, and as we were without arms or supplies, and were furthermore surrounded by the Mexicans far inside their own territory, we could not hope to fight successfully. So [Mangas Coloradas] gave the order to start at once in perfect silence for our homes . . . leaving the dead upon the field.

Completely devastated and suffering from shock, Geronimo watched the others leave. It was as if he were paralyzed. Many of the warriors had lost family members, but all of Geronimo's had been killed. Mangas Coloradas came to him beside the river and together they followed the retreating band. Within a few days they reached their camp in the Gila Mountains.

It was a terrible day for all the Apaches, but Geronimo's life had changed forever. Following Apache custom, he burned all that belonged to his wife and mother. But Geronimo also went beyond what tradition demanded. He burned the playthings of his three children, as well as the tipi he had shared with his family. Later, in his memoirs, Geronimo wrote: "I was never again contented in our happy home, and whenever I saw anything to remind me of former happy days my heart would ache for revenge upon Mexico."

Geronimo had fought the Mexicans since he was a teenager, as had his father and grandfather before him. But the death of his wife and children left him with a personal hatred for the Mexican people that exceeded tribal custom. It also gave him a new, almost magical, strength as a warrior. In Apache terms, the experience brought him a gift of Power from Usen, the Apache god, which would later make him a respected war shaman, or medicine man. In the Apache religion, Power was the name for the life force of the universe. Power was everywhere in the world, but Usen also sent Power to certain individuals in a form that was of specific use in their life. Some men received Power that made them exceptional hunters. Women might receive Power that gave them unusual influence in their family or Power that helped them to bear many children. As the years passed, Power came to Geronimo many times, but the Power he received after the loss of his family was the first such gift from Usen.

At the time, he was sitting alone on a mountain ridge outside of camp, with his head bowed, crying. He heard a voice calling his name. It called four times—a magical number to the Apaches. Then it spoke: "No gun can ever kill you. I will take the bullets from the guns of the Mexicans so they will have nothing but powder. And I will guide your arrows." Geronimo accepted this gift as any Apache would. Throughout his life, he would fight many battles, and though he was often wounded, he would never be killed by an enemy's weapon.

When the survivors of the Janos massacre had recovered, Mangas Coloradas called the warriors together in council to decide what action would be taken against the Mexicans from Sonora. Geronimo had great respect for Mangas Coloradas, as did the rest of the Apache tribe. The great chief was known for many things; he was brave, intelligent, and more than six feet in height, unusually tall for an Apache.

Although each Apache band (a distinct cultural group) operated independently and had its own leaders, bands often came together, either to visit relatives or in times of crisis when called upon by a leader of authority. Mangas Coloradas's influence extended far beyond his own band, the Mimbrenos, and Geronimo's hereditary band, the Bedonkohes. In fact, the great chief of the Chiricahua Apaches, Cochise, was married to one of Mangas Coloradas's daughters.

Thus, when Geronimo joined the council of warriors after the massacre at Janos, he knew his band could count on the support of other Apache groups. He took his place in the circle of warriors and waited while each man in the council was allowed to speak. A decision was made without any arguments: The deaths of their band members must be avenged.

Because Geronimo's personal losses had been so great, the warriors chose him as their representative to enlist the help of their relatives and friends in other bands. Geronimo was not yet a leader, but he was a responsible and trusted warrior, and the others believed in his ability to influence the neighboring groups. The women prepared food for Geronimo to eat on his journey, and the next night he left alone.

First, Geronimo traveled south, to the homeland of the Chiricahuas in the Chiricahua Mountains. There he met Cochise. Like Mangas Coloradas, Cochise was a very powerful chief whose reputation and influence extended over a large territory. Since his childhood, Geronimo had heard stories of Cochise's great fighting ability, but this was the first time he had met the chief. He found that

Cochise was also unusually tall, though not as tall as Mangas Coloradas, and he stood erect, with an air of authority and reserve. Geronimo told Cochise the reason for his visit, and Cochise called a council.

In a remote valley in the mountains, the Chiricahua warriors assembled at dawn to listen to Geronimo. As the eastern sky turned a soft pink, they took their places, sitting on the ground in concentric circles. At a signal from Cochise, Geronimo stepped forward and began his story. With emotion, he told them briefly of the massacre and the losses his band had suffered. Then his sadness turned to bitter anger as he expressed his fierce desire for revenge. He told them about the war party Mangas Coloradas was gathering, calling upon them to join in.

The Chiricahua Mountains in present-day southeastern Arizona was home to the Chiricahuas. The Apaches believed in Mountain Spirits, who were their special protectors.

With confidence and determination, Geronimo promised that he himself would fight as a man with only one purpose. But each warrior must make his own decision. It would be a glorious battle, but whatever the outcome, the warriors must remember that they had come of their own free will.

When Geronimo was finished, he left the camp, and the Chiricahuas talked among themselves. The decision to go to war was not to be made lightly. A battle of the kind Geronimo described would involve many risks. Still, the Mexicans could not go unpunished. If they were allowed to slaughter the Apaches at Janos without paying a price, they might feel free to kill any Apache anywhere. After deliberating for some time, Cochise and the others decided that it was a battle that must be fought for the good of all the Apache people.

Geronimo and Cochise agreed that the Chiricahuas would come to an appointed valley in Mimbreno territory after four moons (about four months) had passed. Then Geronimo continued south to his next destination: the home of the Nednai Apaches, deep in the Sierra Madre, a mountain range in Mexico. The leader of the Nednais was a warrior named Juh. He and Geronimo had been friends since they were boys, and Juh was married to Geronimo's favorite cousin, Ishton. Of all the Apaches, the Nednais were considered the fiercest. Far from any Mexican settlement, their camps were tucked into rocky cliffs and were often difficult to find, even for other Indians. The Nednais had learned to erase any sign of tracks and kept their horses at a safe distance from their camps to avoid detection. Geronimo had spent time with the Nednais when he was an adolescent; his wife had been a Nednai. Although he understood their ways, locating their current camp in the mountains took time and patience.

When Geronimo arrived at last, he was given a warm welcome, which only made it harder for him to deliver his tragic news. Juh was a big, bearlike man, with long hair that hung down his back in braids. He stuttered when he spoke, so he often remained silent, but in his eyes, Geronimo could see sympathy. He could also see that Juh wanted the war almost as much as he did. Geronimo spent a few days mourning with his wife's relatives. Then the warriors assembled, and Geronimo once again recounted the details of the massacre and the reprisal planned by Mangas Coloradas. It was not long before the Nednais also decided to join the attack. Juh promised to come to the land of the Mimbrenos with his warriors at the same time as Cochise. Soon after, Geronimo returned home.

The Apaches often sat in concentric circles when they met in council. The older, more experienced men sat in the inner circles, and the young apprentice warriors occupied the outer circles.

When the four months had passed, hundreds of Apaches began to appear in the designated valley. It was a secluded spot, strategically chosen to hide the large combined force from the Mexicans.

The group would attack a town in Sonora called Arizpe. It was commonly known that the soldiers who massacred Geronimo's family were stationed at Arizpe. The town also was fairly large so that the Apaches could be sure to kill enough Mexicans to avenge their own losses. After everyone had been told the plan, a special area was selected where the women and children would be safely hidden while the warriors were away.

Geronimo and the others in the war party felt they carried the blessing of Usen as they prepared for their journey to Arizpe. Traveling in three divisions—the Mimbrenos and Bedonkohes under Mangas Coloradas, the Chiricahuas under Cochise, and the Nednais under Juh— the Apaches headed south into Sonora. With incredible speed and stealth, they made their way along hidden valleys and rivers on foot because horses would have attracted too much attention. Even in such rough terrain they covered up to 45 miles a day, sometimes running or walking for 14 hours at a time with only short pauses to eat or rest. Driven by his hatred for the Mexicans, Geronimo kept up the fastest pace of all.

Located in a narrow valley along the Sonora River, Arizpe was an ideal target for the Apaches. Geronimo was chosen by the group to direct the fighting. Remembering that day, he said, "I was no chief and never had been, but because I had been more deeply wronged than the others, this honor was conferred upon me, and I resolved to prove worthy of the trust." It would be Geronimo's first major test as a military strategist.

At his order, the warriors approached from the east, where the rugged mountains towered high above the town. The warriors would therefore be hidden until they wanted to be seen. Geronimo also knew that because the closest neighboring town was several miles away, it would be impossible for reinforcements to arrive in time to help the people of Arizpe. He ordered a few of the warriors to make themselves visible to the townspeople, and soon a party of eight Mexican soldiers came out to meet with the Indians. The sight of the Apaches had thrown the town into a flurry of activity, as the men prepared to fight and the women hid their children in shelters. The soldiers hoped that there would be no more than the handful of warriors they had seen, but they knew that most likely they were riding into an ambush. Their priests prayed for them as they left the safety of the town walls, loaded down with gifts for the Indians.

As soon as the soldiers were out of sight of the town, Geronimo's men killed them quickly. He realized that when the Mexicans failed to return, the rest of the troops would follow. The next day, just as he expected, a large force came out to attack. The Apaches were waiting for them.

The battle lasted two hours. Geronimo fought with passion, the memory of his murdered mother, wife, and children always in his mind. First he shot his arrows from behind the trees, picking off a Mexican soldier with each one. When his arrows were gone, he moved in close so he could use his spear, and when that was buried in the body of a Mexican, he continued to fight with only his knife.

To the stunned Mexicans, the young warrior seemed fearless. They began to watch for him in the confusion, calling to each other in terror wherever he appeared, "Watch out! Geronimo!" It is still unclear why—one theory holds that the Mexicans were calling on Saint Jerome to protect them. But from that day the name

Geronimo was chosen to lead the Apaches in their attack on Arizpe. He later explained his strategy: "I arranged the Indians in a hollow circle near the river. . . . We were undercover in the timber. . . . Soon I led the charge . . . at the same time sending some braves to attack [the Mexicans'] rear."

belonged to the young warrior. The Mexicans would recall his fury well in the years to come, and he would always be known as Geronimo. In time the Apaches used the name too, instead of Goyahkla, his birth name. Whereas the Mexicans had shouted the name in fear, many warriors took to yelling the word as they rode into battle. Nearly a hundred years later, American paratroopers in World War II would also use it as a battle cry, shouting "Geronimo!" as they jumped from their planes.

Covered with blood and sweat, Geronimo killed the last of the Mexican soldiers with his knife. The Apaches lost many warriors in the battle at Arizpe, but their losses were small compared to the number of Mexicans they left strewn over the battlefield. Most of the Apaches were satisfied with the outcome. But Geronimo's desire for revenge against Mexico was to last him a lifetime.

The Gila River in the mid-19th century. Geronimo was born near this river at a time when the Apaches were enjoying a rare period of peace.

2

"WARMED BY THE SUN, ROCKED BY THE WINDS"

Geronimo was born near the Gila River in what is now southeastern Arizona, then a part of Mexico. Although there is some discrepancy over the year of Geronimo's birth, the most reliable sources agree that it was about 1823. His mother, Juana, was a Bedonkohe Apache. His father, Taklishim, a Nednai, was required by Apache custom to join his wife's band upon their marriage. Thus, Geronimo was born a Bedonkohe. His parents named him Goyahkla, which means One Who Yawns. Most Indian names were chosen to describe the person in some way, so perhaps Geronimo was a sleepy baby. Certainly the name did not fit his personality later in his life when he proved himself a tireless warrior.

At the time Geronimo was born, the Apaches were enjoying a period of peace, a rare thing in Apache history. As Geronimo put it later, "I was warmed by the sun, rocked by the winds, and sheltered by the trees. . . . During my childhood, we never saw a missionary or a priest. We never saw a white man. Thus quietly lived the Bedonkohe Apaches." This peace meant that during Geronimo's childhood his band changed location less often than it might have if his people had been at war. His parents

23

lived in a tipi, instead of the lighter wickiup the Apaches built when they moved frequently. The dwelling was positioned near those of his mother's sisters and their families, which included eight children. Although they were his cousins, he called them his brothers and sisters. In fact, in the Apache language the same word is used to denote both siblings and cousins. Geronimo remained very close to this extended family throughout his life.

Because they were at peace, Geronimo's parents could devote much time to teaching him Apache legends and traditions. As soon as he was old enough to understand, he was taught that there was a time before the universe was created. Only one thing existed, and that was Power. Out of this endless Power, Usen created the universe— the sun, the moon, the stars, and the earth itself. But there were many kinds of Power, and they were always in conflict. The idea of forces in conflict throughout the universe was very important to the way Geronimo's people understood the world around them. They believed they were put on the earth along with others who would be their natural enemies. Fighting those enemies was as much a part of their nature as hunting animals for food or having children.

In Apache legend, after Usen created the earth, he made all the creatures, large and small. The first humans created by Usen were White Painted Woman and Killer of Enemies. They in turn had a son, Child of the Water, who fought the monsters on earth so that humans could live safely. Whenever Apache men went to war they believed themselves to be enacting the role of Child of the Water, the defender of the human beings.

Geronimo's parents also taught him about the Mountain Spirits, special protectors of the Apache people, who came out of their secret hideouts in mountain caverns to give advice and to help with ceremonies. The Apaches'

Apache women wove baskets that were used in harvesting crops and for storing food. As a boy, Geronimo helped his mother tend their crops.

belief in the Mountain Spirits was one reason they felt so strongly connected to their homeland. When an Apache group was separated from its native mountains it was unprotected by these supernatural beings, who were put on earth by Usen to help them. Geronimo felt the comforting presence of the Mountain Spirits often when he was a child. And many years later, when he was barred from his homeland by U.S. authorities, he would feel the pain of that separation as keenly as any Apache.

Along with his religious education, Geronimo spent many happy hours with his mother learning to tend crops in their vegetable plot. In the spring they planted corn, beans, and pumpkins, and in the autumn they collected the harvest in large baskets woven by the women. When the corn was shelled, it was stored inside a cave, and the entrance was sealed with mud so that the crop would stay fresh over the winter. Geronimo also helped in the making of *tiswin*, an alcoholic drink derived from corn.

The hoop-and-pole game was a popular sport for Apache boys. Each player tried to slide a pole toward a rolling hoop so that when the hoop toppled over, it would rest on the end of the pole.

With his father's guidance, Geronimo learned to make tools and weapons, cared for the family's horses, and practiced using his first bow and arrow. Kneeling beside his young son, Taklishim told him of his own father, Mahko, who had been the chief of the Nednais and a skilled warrior. Though Geronimo never knew his grandfather (he died before Taklishim married), the boy loved to hear stories about him, especially tales about his battles with the Mexicans, who at that time were under Spanish rule. He imagined Mahko as an enormous man with great strength, the kind of man who was not afraid of anything. Mahko had also been rich by Apache standards, due in part to his ability at raiding. He had enough horses and other wealth to afford two wives and a big family. The more stories he heard, the more Geronimo felt his grandfather's blood in his own veins and hoped that someday he too would be a respected leader.

As Geronimo and the other boys in the band grew older, their fathers began the long, arduous task of training them in the ways of an Apache warrior. They were required to develop many different skills. Extreme physical stamina and strength were very important, but so were mental and emotional discipline, an intimate understanding of nature, and a spiritual appreciation for the warrior philosophy.

Every day, Taklishim woke Geronimo before sunrise and watched while he bathed in the icy waters of a nearby river. This would develop his tolerance for cold. Then he practiced dodging, hiding, tracking, and running. The ability to run long distances was a skill that saved the life of many Apaches—men, women, and children. After Geronimo was able to sprint four miles up and down a mountain in the hot sun, his father made him go the whole way with a mouthful of water. He was not

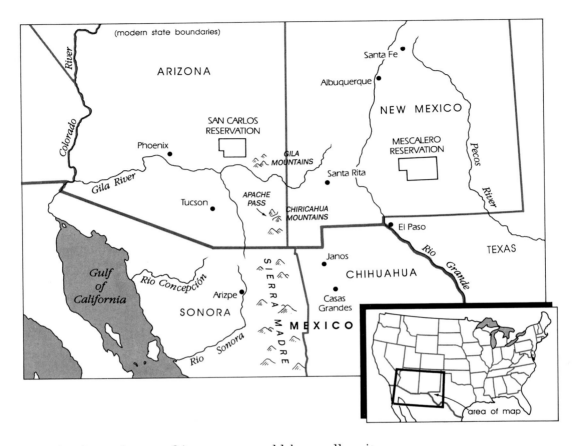

permitted to spit any of it out, nor could he swallow it. This was a test of discipline as well as a way to teach Geronimo to breathe properly, through his nose.

For the most part, Geronimo enjoyed his training, perhaps because he showed a talent for warfare even as a child. With his male cousins and the other boys in camp, he participated in contests of all kinds—wrestling, racing, riding horses, and shooting with a bow and arrow. Geronimo played and fought hard, and liked to win.

By the time he was 10 or 11, Geronimo also hunted with the men. "This was never work," he said later. On the prairies that surrounded their mountains, the Apaches hunted the abundant antelope, elk, deer, and buffalo. On horseback, riding close to the running animals, the Indians shot them with arrows or stabbed them with their spears. These animals provided not only food but also skins that were used as blankets and tipi covers.

Geronimo was already a strong young man when a party of Nednai Apaches from the Sierra Madre came to visit his people. Among them was Juh. He was a stocky youth who always seemed ready to start a fight, perhaps because his stutter embarrassed him. When a group of Bedonkohe girls went into the woods to gather acorns, Juh and his friends waited until their baskets were full and then stole them. One of the girls was Ishton, Geronimo's cousin. Perhaps Juh was just trying to get her attention (he later married her), but this rough play angered Geronimo's grandmother. She told Geronimo to follow Juh and his friends and give them a good beating. As always, Geronimo obeyed her. But instead of making an enemy, he and Juh found they had much in common and became close friends. This friendship would last their entire life.

When Geronimo was about 15, his father died after a long illness. Geronimo's loss was enormous because, not yet a fully grown man, he still needed his father's guidance. Nevertheless, he was not alone, and in the weeks that followed, he became more attached to his family than ever. Soon, Geronimo began to take over the care of his mother, who never remarried, and some of the younger family members. Now when he went hunting with the older warriors, it was not for fun but to provide for his relatives. This new responsibility was difficult at first because Geronimo loved freedom. But when he saw that he was capable of supporting the family, it became a source of pride.

When he felt confident enough, Geronimo decided to take his family on a trip to visit Juh and Ishton among

the Nednais. Juana was still grieving over the loss of
Taklishim, and Geronimo hoped a change of scene would
restore her spirits. The trip would also be a test of his
training. Until that time Geronimo had not experienced
the hostility between the Apaches and the Mexicans
firsthand, though he had certainly been told about it.
Leading the small group deep into Mexico, he took every
precaution he had been taught.

Inside his own territory Geronimo knew the locations
of every water hole and hidden canyon, but on this trip
he had to find water by climbing to a high place and
looking around for green areas. When he found them, he
would go there only at night, when the chance of enemies
arriving there at the same time would be reduced. When
they stopped for rest, he and his family did not sleep
under trees because there they would be easy prey for
wild animals. Instead they chose a place that was
somewhat in the open, but where they might hide
beneath a bush or in high grass.

After spending several frustrating days looking for the
Nednai camp, Geronimo decided to send a smoke signal.
He made a fire, then quickly put it out and hid nearby
to see if anyone would come. Soon a Nednai warrior came
to investigate, and by communicating through birdcalls,
Geronimo told him they were friends of his people. At
last the exhausted travelers were reunited with their
relatives, who held a special feast in their honor.

With the Nednais, Geronimo finally got the opportunity to go on the raids he had dreamed of as a boy.
According to the tribe's tradition, teenage boys decided
for themselves when they were ready to join the men on
raids. And Geronimo was as eager to join the warriors as
any young man the Nednais had ever seen.

Like any Apache, he began as an apprentice. The older
men trained him and his fellow apprentices and, in

return, the youths did all the work around the camp: taking care of the horses, cooking, gathering wood, and standing guard. If they showed themselves to be brave and dependable on four expeditions, they were then allowed to join the council of warriors.

Geronimo went with Juh, who by this time was the leader of the Nednais. Together they raided Mexican ranches and pack trains and made off with horses, mules, and other supplies. Sometimes they also killed the Mexicans who tried to defend their possessions. But Geronimo was to learn that there was a big difference between war and raiding. The purpose of war was to kill enemies; the purpose of a raid was to seize enemy property and get away unharmed. During a raid, a warrior had to exercise extreme caution and avoid conflict, and even discovery, whenever possible. An otherwise successful raid might be considered a disaster if a warrior was killed.

Geronimo took to raiding easily. Though he was only five feet, eight inches tall, he was powerfully built, extremely quick on his feet, and skilled with all of the Apache weapons. Geronimo loved the excitement, the challenge, and, most of all, the glory of bringing home the spoils to his family. Every successful raid was followed by a feast and much dancing and singing. Geronimo had always loved these celebrations, but now they brought an added pleasure: a slender, delicate young girl named Alope with whom he had fallen in love. Her parents watched them closely, as did all Apache parents of unmarried girls, but at a feast he was at least allowed to dance as her partner.

Geronimo's confidence and enthusiasm served him well. He was accepted as a warrior, and with this new position came the right to marry. Wasting no time, Geronimo went to Alope's father and prepared to negotiate for her. Alope too was eligible to marry, having

Depiction of a womanhood ceremony, painted on buckskin. Each of the girls has an older woman as an attendant. In the middle of the painting are dancers "worshiping" the fire.

completed her own womanhood ceremony—a four-day celebration given by her parents.

Alope's father was not surprised that Geronimo wanted his daughter, for he had known of their attraction to each other for some time. But among the Apaches it was customary for the young man's parents, or another representative, to call on the girl's parents. The young warrior was expected to wait outside, and the girl to sit inside, neither permitted to speak, while the parents discussed the terms of the marriage settlement. But Geronimo would have none of this. He appeared at the tipi of Alope's father and announced his intention to marry her. After several moments of silence, her father asked in return a large number of ponies. In his memoirs, Geronimo wrote, "I made no reply, but in a few days appeared before him with the herd of ponies and took with me Alope. This was all the marriage ceremony necessary in our tribe."

A few weeks later, Alope, Geronimo, and his mother moved back to Bedonkohe territory, where he built a new home for his young wife. As an old man, he remembered her as "a good wife, but never strong. We followed the traditions of our fathers and were happy. Three children came to us—children that played, loitered, and worked as I had done."

Geronimo's peaceful family life ended suddenly when Alope and his children were killed at Janos. But he was not alone in his suffering. The Apaches had been at war with the Mexicans for so long that there was none among them who had not lost a relative to violence.

The Mexican town of Arizpe,
which the Apaches attacked in
response to the massacre at
Janos one year earlier.

3

MEXICANS AND AMERICANS

Under Sonoran colonel Jose Carrasco, the 400 Mexican troops at Janos had killed 21 Indians and taken 62 captives to sell as slaves. As far as Carrasco was concerned, he was avenging many years of raids and deaths inflicted by the Apaches. From 1831 to 1849, 26 mines, 39 small settlements, and 98 ranches were abandoned in Sonora. Citizens were leaving the area in droves. Some headed for California, after gold was discovered there in 1848, but many left out of fear of Apache attacks.

The Mexican government had taken few steps to protect them. The late 1840s had been a time of anarchy in Mexico. From 1846 to 1848, the country had been at war with the United States over control of the land that is now Texas. The war cost Mexico dearly. According to the peace agreement, the Treaty of Guadalupe Hidalgo, Mexico surrendered much of its northern territory to the United States. The war also left the country near bankruptcy and unable to deal effectively with the Apaches. For decades the Mexican states of Chihuahua and Sonora established separate policies regarding the Indians. At varying times, both issued scalp bounties, paying 100 pesos for the scalp of an Apache warrior, 50 for that of a woman, and 25 for that of a child. But in 1849, Chihuahua decided to try peace for a while. And, in fact, the Indians massacred at Janos were supposedly under the Chihuahua government's protection.

Carrasco returned to Sonora a hero, but to the Chihuahua authorities, his crossing of the state border to attack the Apaches was a criminal act that upset their hopes for peace. They complained to authorities in Mexico City, the capital of Mexico. However, Carrasco presented evidence that supplies recovered from the Indians' camp belonged to citizens of Sonora, and the Mexican government took his side in the matter. While the Indians quietly made their plans for revenge, Carrasco grew confident that his attack had finally defeated them. The battle at Arizpe proved him very wrong.

When the last Mexican soldier on the field at Arizpe was dead, the Apache warriors slipped quietly back into the mountains. Cautiously, they made their way to the hidden campground where their families waited, stopping often to watch for signs of pursuit. But except for a handful of soldiers who soon got lost, no one followed. It had been a glorious victory that would be retained in Apache history as a favorite story, passed from father to son.

Once reunited, the warriors, women, and children mourned their losses and celebrated their successful revenge. Then Cochise and Juh returned with their people to their own homeland. For them the mission was over. But Geronimo found it very difficult to put his desire for vengeance behind him. It had sustained him for more than a year following the death of his family, and when he was not fighting, he felt a deep sense of emptiness.

Geronimo's remaining relatives stayed together and often looked to him for advice and support. Soon,

One of Geronimo's wives and two of their children. In keeping with his increasing prominence among the Apaches, Geronimo expanded his number of spouses.

Geronimo married again and then took another wife, a sign of his rising status in the band and his ability to support a large family. The two wives were Bedonkohes. The first, named Chee-hash-kish, would bear him a son, Chappo, and a daughter, Dohn-say. The second was Nana-tha-thtith, and she had one child. Members of his new family would be at his side through many battles in the years ahead.

As much as he loved his family, Geronimo spent little time in camp, preferring to return to raid and kill in

Mexico. Although he had proven his fighting ability at Arizpe and had won the respect of his people, he was only about 27 years old. He was driven to fight but lacked the caution and good judgment of a more seasoned warrior. For the next year, when Geronimo went raiding, his failures outnumbered his successes. He was injured twice, once in the head, and the wounds took a long time to heal.

Mangas Coloradas did not approve of Geronimo's Mexican raids, but he did not forbid him to go. No Apache chief would presume to tell a warrior how to live, and in Geronimo's case, Mangas Coloradas knew there was little chance of changing his mind. Although Mangas Coloradas hated the Mexicans as much as Geronimo, he preferred not to fight if possible. He had become known for his peaceful solutions when arbitrating differences among his people. Soon the chief's philosophy of peace was tested in a bigger arena.

In the summer of 1851, a boundary commission, made up of both Americans and Mexicans, arrived to mark off the new international border between the United States and Mexico. Leading the commission was John Bartlett for the Americans and General Pedro Conde for the Mexicans. John Cremony, a young newspaper reporter from Boston who spoke fluent Spanish, came along as the interpreter. And a military escort was included to protect the party.

In the middle of the Mimbrenos' territory there was a copper mine and an adjoining settlement called Santa Rita. The settlement had been run by Mexicans until it was abandoned in 1838 following an incident in which a treacherous scalp hunter killed many Apaches, including members of Mangas Coloradas's family. Bartlett chose Santa Rita as his base of operations and had already moved in when Mangas Coloradas returned from the battle at Arizpe. These men were the first whites Geronimo had ever seen. Although he personally had little to do with the commissioners, their interactions with Mangas Coloradas are an important example of the many problems the Indians encountered when trying to cooperate with the Americans—even a relatively reasonable American such as Bartlett.

Relations started out peacefully enough. Mangas Coloradas, with a few warriors, paid Bartlett a visit and asked what he was doing. Bartlett explained about the war between the United States and Mexico and the terms of the Treaty of Guadalupe Hidalgo. He told Mangas Coloradas that because the Indians were now on U.S. land, the Americans would protect them if they behaved, but they were also bound by the treaty to protect the

U.S. boundary commissioner John Bartlett was fair minded and believed that if the Indians were treated justly, they would respond in kind.

Mexicans from Apache attacks across the border. Mangas Coloradas argued that they had no right to restrict the Apaches, and that the Apaches had always fought the Mexicans and would continue to do so. After all, the Americans themselves had fought the Mexicans. As to the land, Usen had created it for the Mimbrenos, but they did not mind the small group of strangers sharing it temporarily. He agreed to let Bartlett go about his business. Bartlett, fearing an attack, pressed no further.

For a few weeks, Mangas Coloradas kept his promise to leave the commission in peace. And another group, the Warm Springs Apaches, who came into the area and camped on the Mimbres River below Santa Rita, were friendly as well. Survey parties went out 50 miles in each direction and came back with no trouble. Wagons full of food for the base camp arrived safely. The commission even brought in a herd of cattle, which grazed undisturbed in the fields near the abandoned mine.

Then one day, two young Mexican boys, whom the Warm Springs Apaches had taken captive years before and had raised as their own children, ran away and hid in Cremony's tent. Cremony turned the boys over to General Conde, who sent them back to their families in Mexico. The Apaches were greatly angered at this and quickly held a council.

Accompanied by Delgadito of the Warm Springs Apaches, and about 200 warriors, Mangas Coloradas confronted Bartlett and asked why the captives were taken from them. Cremony later recorded Mangas Coloradas's words in his book *Life Among the Apaches*:

> You came to our country. You were well received. Your lives, your property, your animals were safe. Our wives and our children came here and visited your houses. We were friends. We were brothers! Believing this, we came among you and brought our captives. . . . We believed your assurances of friendship, and we trusted them.

Copper mines at Santa Rita, which flourished as a mining town in the first half of the 19th century.

Bartlett then tried to explain the new relationship between the United States and Mexico:

> I have no doubt that you have suffered much by the Mexicans. This is a question in which it is impossible for us to tell who is right, or who is wrong. You and the Mexicans accuse each other of being the aggressors. Our duty is to fulfil our promise to both . . . to show Mexico that we mean what we say; and when the time comes . . . to prove the good faith of our promises to you.

Delgadito listened carefully and said that he understood Bartlett's position, but there must also be justice for the warrior who lost the captives, after obtaining them "at the risk of his life and with the blood of his relatives."

With the Mimbrenos camped on one side of Santa Rita and the Warm Springs group on the other, Bartlett knew he had better find a way to keep the Indians happy. It was against military policy to ransom captives, but he chose to ignore this and offered to pay for the boys. The Apaches left to consult among themselves, and when they returned, Delgadito said, "The brave who owns these captives does not want to sell. He has had one of those boys six years. . . . He is a son to his old age. He speaks our language. He loves the boy and cannot sell him." Bartlett eventually persuaded the Apaches to accept $250 worth of blankets and brightly colored cloth, but it was clear that they still felt mistreated.

A few days later, a Mexican working for the boundary commission shot and killed an Apache warrior for no reason. The Indians wanted him publicly executed. In keeping with U.S. law, Bartlett intended to send the murderer to Santa Fe, in present-day New Mexico, for trial. But he promised to turn the man's wages over to the victim's mother. In keeping with Apache law, she said she wanted blood, not money. Finally the matter was settled by arranging to give her the prisoner's back wages as well as the monthly wage he would earn by working in chains. But again, although Bartlett thought the arrangement pleased the Indians, it did not.

These two incidents were followed by others that demonstrated to the Apaches that the boundary commission had only its own interests in mind and could not be trusted. Little by little, commission mules and supplies began to disappear. After several small skirmishes with the Indians, Bartlett was forced to bring in the surveying parties and place a guard around the settlement. Not long after, he left Santa Rita and continued west.

Meanwhile, a new group of prospectors began to work the mines at Santa Rita. These men were greedy and violent and cared little for the rights of the Apaches. Soon, the Indians retaliated by raiding their settlement and killing travelers.

In July 1852, after many incidents of Apache violence, John Greiner, who was the government official in charge of Indian affairs in New Mexico Territory, decided the situation had gotten out of hand. He called Mangas Coloradas and other leaders to Sante Fe and made a treaty with them. The United States promised to provide the Indians with gifts, treat them well, and punish American citizens who harmed them. The Apaches in turn agreed to allow the Americans free passage through their territory. The treaty also committed the Apaches to stop raiding in Mexico, but because they verbally disagreed with this provision at the time the treaty was signed, they did not consider it binding.

Greiner's treaty kept the peace between the Apaches and the Americans for several years, but raids in Mexico continued, as did Mexican attacks on the Apaches. In one such case, Geronimo was in camp, recuperating from injuries, when three companies of Mexican soldiers surprised them. Most of the warriors were away trading with the Navajo Indians who lived to the northwest. Many women and children died in the attack, including Geronimo's wife Nana-tha-thtith and her child. The troopers burned their tipis and carried off their ponies, weapons, food, and blankets. Four women were also taken captive, to be sold as slaves in Sonora.

With the death of another wife and child to avenge, Geronimo was full of fresh hatred for the Mexicans. He continued his relentless raiding. The following summer, he captured a long pack train loaded with blankets, calico cloth, saddles, tinware, and sugar. When the warriors returned home, Mangas Coloradas brought several groups together to celebrate with feasting and all-night dancing.

Considered a cruel and blood-thirsty savage by non-Indians, Geronimo saw his actions merely as retaliation for wrongs inflicted upon him and his people. Here he wears on his collar two molded Mexican silver dollars.

His days of failure well behind him, Geronimo, commanding increasingly large groups of warriors, continued to bring home large quantities of food, horses, and supplies. On one occasion, he captured a herd of cattle, the first his people had ever seen. They killed the entire herd, dried the beef, and dressed the hides. The animals provided enough food to last almost an entire year.

Around this time, some American prospectors discovered gold in Mimbreno territory. The town of Pinos Altos sprang up almost overnight, full of miners with no regard for the Indians. Foolishly, these miners even invited Mexicans to come in and farm near their settlement to give the prospectors a cheap source of food. Of course this was a direct affront to the Apaches, and it led to several hostile clashes.

Although the Mimbrenos obtained food through raiding, they were suffering greatly from a loss of game in their territory. Hoping to reestablish peace so that his people could concentrate on surviving, Mangas Coloradas went alone to Pinos Altos, although Geronimo pleaded with him not to trust the miners. Geronimo was right. The miners tied Mangas Coloradas to a tree and beat him severely with bullwhips. When the ordeal was over, the great chief crept away and hid while his wounds healed. No one had ever hit him like that before, and the humiliation was devastating. Mangas Coloradas would never again trust Americans. A few months later he collected Apaches from the surrounding country, including his son-in-law Cochise, and waged a long, bloody war that eventually drove the miners out.

Meanwhile, American traffic had increased on the California Trail, a route that led through Mimbreno country and south into the Chiricahua Mountains, where Cochise's band was located. With Cochise's permission, a rest station was built near an important water source in

a place that would come to be called Apache Pass. In 1858, the Butterfield Stage Line began to travel the route twice a week, carrying mail and passengers from St. Louis to San Francisco.

By this time, Geronimo and his Bedonkohe relatives were spending much of their time with the Chiricahuas, perhaps because Geronimo had married a Chiricahua-Nednai woman named She-gha. Then, sometime later,

A Butterfield mail coach in the early 1860s. At first, Cochise allowed the stage line to traverse his band's territory unmolested. However, the Cut the Tent Affair put an end to the initial peace between Cochise and the whites.

he took another wife, a Bedonkohe named Shtsha-she.

As Mangas Coloradas had done before him, Cochise began his relations with the Americans he met at Apache Pass on a friendly note. One winter he even had a contract to supply the station with wood. But another unfortunate incident would soon make him hate the "white eyes" as much as Mangas did. The affair started when a young half-Mexican boy was abducted from his family's ranch nearby.

The boy's father assumed that he had been taken by the Chiricahuas (this later proved untrue) and complained to the American military. The army sent Second Lieutenant George Bascom, a brash young officer with little experience, to Apache Pass to recover him. Responding to a summons from Bascom, Cochise, his wife, his young son Naiche, a brother, and two nephews arrived at the station. Bascom invited them into his tent, and then demanded the stolen boy. Cochise said he did not have the child but promised to find him if possible. Bascom called the chief a liar and threatened to hold him hostage until the boy was returned.

Cochise took out his knife, sliced a hole in the wall of the tent, and escaped. But Bascom still held the other Indians, and in an effort to get them back, Cochise captured three men from the station and offered to exchange prisoners. Bascom refused, saying he would not negotiate until Cochise brought him the boy.

Sure that his family was as good as dead, Cochise killed his hostages about a month later. Bascom let Cochise's wife and Naiche go, but hung his brother and two nephews. Known as the Cut the Tent Affair among the Apaches, this event was to infuriate Indian groups throughout the Southwest. The incident marked the end of peaceful relations and the beginning of a long period of war that would result in many deaths on both sides.

4

A DECADE OF WAR

Lieutenant Bascom had made a grievous mistake when he accused Cochise of stealing the rancher's boy, and the many American settlers who now dotted the Southwest were made to pay for it. Looking for adventure and an opportunity for a new life on the wild frontier, they came mostly from the East and the North—gold prospectors, copper miners, ranchers, and their families. There were many obstacles to overcome. Much of the region was extremely hot during the day and cold at night, and the dry, arid soil was hardly ideal for cultivating crops. But the biggest obstacle had nothing to do with the climate: The Apaches were everywhere, and they were more determined than ever to rid their homeland of the American invaders.

Geronimo fought eagerly. He had come to feel strongly that the best chance the Apaches had of keeping their land and their freedom was relentless war. In a very short time, the Americans had achieved a new status among the Apaches. Like the Mexicans before them, they were now the enemy. Geronimo continually led attacks on the new settlements, stealing their horses and food, and killing anyone who tried to stop him.

Prospectors studying ore. In the mid-19th century, the search for gold lured Americans westward from the East and the North.

In the summer of 1861, the Apaches believed they were finally beating the Americans. The military posts in their territory were evacuated. With their protection gone, the settlers began to leave their homes in the countryside and collect in the larger towns, where they would be less vulnerable to Apache attacks. Naturally, this looked very encouraging to the Indians and only caused them to intensify their raiding and killing. When Geronimo joined Mangas Coloradas or Cochise to celebrate their frequent victories, it seemed that they would soon be rid of the Americans for good. They did not know that the reason the soldiers had left had nothing to do with them. It was the beginning of the American Civil War.

Fought between northern (Union) states and southern (Confederate) states, the Civil War began when the South tried to establish itself as a separate country where slavery would continue to be legal. The war lasted for four bloody years before the South surrendered. Union soldiers in Apache territory were ordered east to defend the South-west from a Confederate attack. They spread throughout the mountains of the Rio Grande, but when the attack came, they were no match for it. Confederate forces overcame them and settled in the city of Sante Fe.

The Confederates had no experience fighting Apaches, however. Soon, the Indians wore down their forces. When they received word that Union general James Carleton was gathering an army of about 1,800 men and preparing to move east through the Arizona Territory, the Con-federates retreated—with the Apaches on their heels making sure they did not change their mind.

Cochise also got word that Carleton's force was coming. When the Union soldiers got as far as Tucson, he enlisted Mangas Coloradas's Mimbrenos and other bands to help him defend Apache Pass. Mangas arrived with more than 200 warriors. These men, combined with Cochise's,

Apache Pass, the scene of a significant battle between the Apaches and the U.S. military. The soldiers used howitzers to rout the Indians, who up to that point in the conflict had been safely hidden behind mountain rocks.

formed a force of about 550 warriors, the largest group the Apaches had ever assembled for war.

Knowing that the American troops would be tired and thirsty after marching for days in the hot sun, Cochise decided to prepare an ambush at the spring near the abandoned Butterfield station. Geronimo took his place with the other warriors in the mountain rocks overlooking the site. This time there were no bows and arrows. All of the warriors were well armed with rifles and ammunition stolen from the whites they had killed.

On July 14, 1862, Apache scouts watched an advance party consisting of 126 Union men, 242 horses, and 26 wagons full of supplies enter the pass. Safe behind enormous rocks, the rest of the warriors waited silently for the marching soldiers to enter the canyon where they could easily be picked off. When the enemy army was within range, they began to shoot, bringing down many of the Union soldiers, whom they called "blue coats." The Union men shot back, but they could hardly see the Apaches, let alone hit them.

In the middle of the battle, the Apaches watched as the soldiers rolled forward two of their wagons. Inside were howitzers—short cannons with enough power to shoot upward at a mountain target. The Apaches had never seen howitzers before, and when the first blast brought rocks sliding down all around them, they were taken completely by surprise. Despite all their careful plans, the stunned Indians had no choice but to withdraw. The battle at Apache Pass was over in less than an hour, but it was an important turning point in the war between the Apaches and the Americans.

Several smaller skirmishes followed, but it seemed that luck was on the side of the soldiers. Mangas Coloradas was seriously wounded while trying to overtake a band of messengers headed back to warn the rest of General Carleton's army. Deeply demoralized by their military failure and in fear of losing their chief, the Apaches made no effort to stop the rest of the California soldiers. The army marched through Apache Pass, stopped for water at the spring, and continued east to fight in the Civil War.

Before leaving the area, General Carleton assigned a detail of soldiers to stay behind and build a fort to guard the spring so that it could be used safely by any Americans traveling the trail. The Apaches could only watch as the

General James Carleton strikes a characteristic pose. He was inflexible, defiant, and merciless in his dealings with the Indians.

men erected stone walls they had no hope of penetrating. Named Fort Bowie after one of the officers who built it, the new military post became a permanent fixture in Chiricahua territory.

When Carleton reached the Rio Grande, he assumed command of New Mexico Territory and established his own rules for dealing with the Indians. He ordered that all Indian men be shot on sight unless they could be easily captured. Within a year, he had rounded up the

become famous in Apache history; Loco, a brave warrior who once killed a grizzly bear single-handedly, and was said to have run through a storm of bullets to rescue a wounded warrior (thus his name, which is Spanish for "crazy"); and Nana, an older, grandfatherly warrior, who

Mescalero Apaches, who lived in the Rio Grande mountains, as well as the Navajos, a tribe that lived a more sedentary life than the Apaches. He put the two tribes on one small reservation, where they fought each other and starved due to a lack of animals to hunt. In the winter

was wise and kind with his own people, but completely merciless when fighting non-Indians. These men were to play an important role in Geronimo's life in the years to come.

When the Civil War ended in 1865, settlers began to return to the area, but the Apaches continued to fight them off, despite the presence of a number of military posts. The Warm Springs band, of which Geronimo was then a member, offered to stop their war if they could have their homeland as a reservation—the first of many such requests made by Victorio, who like Mangas Coloradas, seemed to prefer peace to war. But the valley they wanted most, in truth only a small part of what had once been their territory, was one of the most pleasant and fertile in the region. There were already non-Indian families settled on it. The request was denied, and the wars continued.

In the Chiricahua Mountains, Cochise was also trying to hold back the Americans. Any traveler on the California Trail was risking death. Then he met Thomas Jeffords, a white man who was later to become an important figure in peace negotiations. Jeffords was a mail superintendent, in charge of the route between Fort Bowie and Tucson, in Cochise's territory. During his 18 months on the job he himself was wounded by an Apache arrow, and 14 of his drivers were killed.

Finally, Jeffords decided to visit Cochise personally. He went to the chief's mountain stronghold alone and unarmed. It was the first time since Lieutenant Bascom had hanged his brother and nephews that a white man had seen the formidable chief and lived. Jeffords's bravery impressed Cochise, and the two became good friends, though Cochise continued his war on all other whites.

After living with the Warm Springs Apaches off and on for a few years, Geronimo went back to the

Loco, one of the leaders of the Warm Springs Apaches. This band was so called because its members prized a spring in their homeland that they believed had healing properties.

Chiricahuas. Juh and his wife, Ishton, were living there too, and Geronimo looked forward to seeing them, for he had been separated from them for some time. Geronimo arrived in the winter of 1869, just as the pregnant Ishton was going into labor. Ishton was a remarkable woman, calm, intelligent, and strong, but the labor had already been going on for a full day and was extremely painful. Ishton's child was named Daklugie, which means "he who forced his way through." The child would become one of Geronimo's closest friends and would remain so until the day Geronimo died.

During the 1860s, the United States government had no consistent policy when it came to dealing with the Apaches. Some Indian agents (officials in charge of reservations) and military officers in present-day Arizona and New Mexico attempted to put them on reservations. But because these lands were usually uninhabitable, the Indians did not stay on them. Other whites only wanted to hunt down the Apaches. Meanwhile, the new citizens in the area were complaining vociferously about Apache raids. In Washington, it finally became clear that a solution was needed, but the Department of the Interior, which included the Bureau of Indian Affairs (BIA), and the Department of War were divided over what should be done.

In 1871, the military brought in General George Crook, who had had great success subduing Indians in the Pacific Northwest. Nevertheless, he had a lot to learn about fighting Indians who seemed able to strike a settlement and then disappear completely. As soon as he arrived he made a complete inspection of all the military posts in the territory and interviewed many army personnel and civilians. Little by little he came to develop tactics that would prove effective against the Apaches. He stopped using large supply wagons, which were easy targets for

Apache raids and were cumbersome in the mountains. He replaced them with the much more efficient pack-mule trains. He made his troops fight on foot, instead of on horses, for better mobility. Most important, he enlisted Apache warriors from the reservations to act as scouts.

By the end of these preparations, Crook was so confident, he said, "If this entire Indian question would be left to me . . . I have not the slightest doubt of my ability to conquer a peace with this Apache race in a comparatively short space of time." His tactics were more clever than those previously used by the U.S. military, but, like many before him, Crook had underestimated the Apaches.

Apache scouts in the early 1880s. The U.S. Army enlisted reservation Indians to help locate, pursue, and fight the "renegades."

General Oliver Howard was able to strike a land settlement with Cochise that also pleased Geronimo. Howard was one of the few white men whom Geronimo liked and trusted.

Working quickly, Crook selected several sites to turn into Apache reservations. One was the Tularosa Valley, where some of the Warm Springs Apaches had already lived for a short time. They had suffered greatly from the cold climate, and the impure water in the region had led to much sickness and the death of several children. In December 1871, Crook sent word to the various bands that they must move to their appointed reservations by mid-February or they would be punished. Only a small percentage of the Apaches complied with his order.

Then, in February 1872, just as Crook was about to set out with his troops to round up the others, he was notified that a General Oliver Howard was being sent on a "peace mission" to negotiate with the Indians and establish a "fair" system of reservations. Crook had met Howard before. The man had distinguished himself as an officer in the Civil War and had even lost an arm in battle. He was also very religious and likely to drop to his knees to pray at any given moment. After the Civil War he worked with black people in the South, considering himself to be "the Moses to the Negro." Crook was furious that the pious Howard would be allowed to upset his plans, but there was nothing he could do about it.

Howard made his own inspections, but unlike Crook, he interviewed the Indians themselves, as well as much of the military and civilian population. He made several changes in Crook's reservation assignments to the benefit of the Indians, and then prepared to visit the great Cochise. Victorio, assured that he would finally get the land he wanted, arranged for several men to accompany Howard: Thomas Jeffords, the only white man trusted by Cochise; a young warrior named Chee, who was one of Cochise's nephews; and Ponce, a son of Mangas Coloradas.

When the small party reached Cochise's domain, Chee guided them into a sheltered valley, barking like a coyote and using smoke signals to alert the Chiricahuas that they were coming. The chief was not in camp when they arrived, and it was not clear whether the general would be welcomed or killed.

Cochise kept Howard waiting almost a full day; then he rode in, with his wife, his sister, and his young son Naiche. He greeted Jeffords warmly and shook Howard's hand. When everyone was seated, he began to describe the incident of the stolen boy and his subsequent war with the whites. Then he said, "I have retaliated with all my might. I have killed ten white men for every Indian slain. But now I am ready to make peace."

Cochise then sent for Geronimo and other leading warriors and began to negotiate a settlement. Howard remained in the camp for 11 days and made every effort to create a good impression. Finally, Howard and Cochise agreed on a Chiricahua reservation 70 square miles in size. The terms meant Cochise would give up a vast amount of land, which he knew would be lost forever, but in the end, the small portion of Chiricahua homeland was enough. At least this land was to be theirs for all time, it seemed. Cochise also stipulated that Thomas Jeffords must serve as agent on the reservation. And although this was a lot of responsibility for Jeffords, who had never worked with the Indians in an official capacity, he accepted the job in the interest of peace.

Geronimo was also pleased with the agreement. Even he liked Howard. As Howard and Cochise were preparing to leave to tell the military at Fort Bowie about the treaty, Geronimo made an unusual gesture of trust, and asked the general if he could ride with him on his horse. According to the general's journal, Geronimo put his hands on the horse's hind quarters, sprang up from behind, and put his arms around him. The two got to be friends on the ride, though when they got near the fort, the general felt Geronimo tremble.

His mission accomplished, General Howard returned to Washington, leaving Crook behind to deal with any stray raiding Apaches. This Crook did with amazing effectiveness, acquiring a new name in the process. The Apaches called him Nantan Lupan, or Gray Wolf. Though they considered him a tough enemy, they learned that at least he never lied to them.

But for the most part, the Chiricahuas, including Geronimo, lived peacefully on their new reservation.

Although some of the warriors continued to raid in Mexico, Cochise discouraged them whenever possible, and on the American side of the border he made every effort to protect the ranchers and travelers, even from other Indians, so that he could not be accused of failing to keep his word. For his part, Jeffords secured clothing, rations, and supplies for his charges, which cut down on their need to raid.

Though they were confined within the boundaries set by the treaty, the Apaches on the Chiricahua reservation were generally able to live according to their traditional ways. Small groups settled in different areas, and then came together as they wished—for celebrations or just to visit. There were animals to hunt, and believing that they would be on the land forever, the Apaches on the reservation planted crops again, as they had done nearly 30 years before, when Geronimo was a boy.

Apaches digging an irrigation canal at the San Carlos reservation in the 1880s. In the mid-1870s, the U.S. government decided to consolidate the Indians in present-day central Arizona at this reservation.

5

ARREST AND TRIAL

In 1875, the U.S. government instituted a new policy for dealing with the Indians who were living on reservations in the American Southwest. It was known as consolidation. Instead of allowing different groups to stay on their own reservations, as agreed by General Howard three years earlier, officials in Washington decided to move all the Apaches to San Carlos, a large reservation in the middle of what is now Arizona. Assembling all the Indians in the region in one place would make them easier to control, the government reasoned. In addition, the American citizens in present-day Arizona and New Mexico wanted the Indians' land for their settlements. It would make no difference that some of the tribes assigned to San Carlos were hostile to each other. Nor did it matter that San Carlos was mostly desert, covered with rocks and overrun with rattlesnakes.

Cochise got sick and died the year before the new policy was to go into effect. Before his death, he called his top warriors to his side and told them that he was designating Taza, his eldest son, as his successor. Taza had been carefully trained for this responsibility, and Cochise asked him and his younger brother, Naiche, to promise to keep the peace with the Americans. But Taza's influence was not as strong as his father's. Though many remained loyal to him, some of the warriors in the band would not abide by his decisions. They left the reservation and began raiding in the surrounding territory.

John Clum, the agent at San Carlos, had already spent a year uprooting different bands and taking them back to his reservation. In June 1876, he arrived at Fort Bowie with an armed guard and prepared to do the same with the Chiricahuas. Taza met with Clum and listened to his explanation of the new policy. The idea that his people would have to leave their land was a terrible blow to the young Apache trying so hard to fulfill his new role as chief. Taza tried to reason with Clum, telling him of the treaty with Howard, but finally he decided that he had no choice but to go. If he tried to fight, many of his people would probably be killed, and his father had asked him to keep the peace.

In another camp about 20 miles away, Geronimo got word that armed men had come to remove the Indians. Accompanied by two warriors, he rode to Fort Bowie and asked to talk to the officer in charge. Again, Clum explained the new policy. For a moment Geronimo was sad. It seemed even General Howard's word was not enough to protect the Apaches.

In fact, General Howard—and General Crook—had strongly opposed consolidating the Apache reservations. It was probably the only time the two ever agreed. Both could see that removing the Indians from their land just as they were settling down, and only a few years after they had been told it would be theirs "forever," was surely asking for trouble.

Geronimo questioned Clum about the new reservation, and then, seemingly satisfied, announced that he would go but first he needed a little time to return to his camp and gather his people together. Clum agreed but, suspecting that Geronimo might be lying, sent two scouts to follow him. When Geronimo got back to his encampment he ordered his people to prepare to leave immediately. By the time the scouts reported back to Clum, the band was long gone. From then on, Geronimo would be known as a "renegade" Indian.

Later, Geronimo pointed out that his agreement had been with Howard, not Clum. He said in his memoirs, "I do not think that I ever belonged to those soldiers at Apache Pass, or that I should have asked them where I might go."

The reservation at San Carlos had been considered a hellish place from the beginning. There was little game for the Apaches to hunt and almost no trees. It also had a history of being run by swindlers who withheld the

An 1890 cartoon lampooning the corrupt Indian agents. Here the agent has given the Indian a small package of "starvation rations" while he keeps what should have rightly gone to his reservation charges.

Indians' rations and treated them unjustly. But Clum was basically honorable, and when he took over, he set up several progressive systems that improved the atmosphere of the place considerably.

He reduced the number of soldiers stationed there and set up an Indian court, with the chiefs as judges. The Indians appreciated his ability to recognize that they had their own laws and should be judged by their own people, not by the whites. Clum also trained warriors as police and gave them blue uniforms to wear. And every week, he called in all the Indians on the reservation to be counted, so that if they were falsely accused of raiding they would have an alibi. As one Apache later said, "As agents went, John Clum was one of the best."

Nevertheless, when it came to Geronimo, Clum's understanding and fairness disappeared. The Apache had made a fool of him, and from that time on he blamed every raid that was reported on Geronimo, whether he had committed the crime or not. Soon, civilians began to blame Geronimo as well. It was not long before his name was known in every household in present-day Arizona.

There were more than 100 men, women, and children with Geronimo when he fled the Chiricahua reservation, including Juh and Ishton. When the group was far enough away that they felt it was safe to stop and rest, the warriors held a council. They decided that Juh would lead the Nednais back to their homeland in the Sierra Madre, and Geronimo would take the remainder of the group to the Warm Springs reservation.

When his band arrived there, they found that other Apaches who had been ordered to go to San Carlos under the consolidation policy had escaped as well. In fact, the Warm Springs reservation had become a hideout for 135 renegades. There was no way the rations meant for the Warm Springs band would feed the entire group. Furthermore, the authorities who were supposed to be managing the reservation chose to ignore the additional Indians rather than attempt to control them. Soon, the renegades began to steal horses from ranchers in Arizona Territory and sell them to ranchers in New Mexico Territory. For a few months, it was an easy way for them to get food and supplies.

In March 1877, the commissioner of Indian affairs (the official in charge of the BIA) wired from Washington ordering Clum to go to the Warm Springs reservation and arrest the renegades. He was to take them to San Carlos and charge them with robbery and murder. Three companies of cavalry would be sent to meet him. Clum arrived in April with 100 of his Indian police and then decided not to wait for the cavalry. His son later wrote a book about Clum's experiences with the Apaches called *Apache Agent: The Story of John P. Clum.* In it, he described what happened the day his father arrested Geronimo.

Knowing that a large number of Indians in uniforms would scare off the Apache warriors, Clum brought the police in at night and hid all but 22 of them in an abandoned adobe building near the reservation headquarters. At dawn, he sent a messenger to Geronimo and the other renegade leaders who were camped about three miles away, inviting them to come in for a conference. The messenger seemed friendly, so Geronimo did not expect a fight. He arrived with six other leaders and a group of women and children. As Geronimo approached the headquarters building, Clum came out and stood on the porch. Three Indian police stood on either side of him; 16 more waited in front of the other buildings in the small compound. Geronimo had heard of Clum's Indian police, but this was the first time he saw them for himself, and they made him feel strange.

With the other leaders, Geronimo walked up to Clum and asked him what he wanted. Clum answered that he had come to charge Geronimo with stealing cattle and horses and killing American citizens, thereby breaking the peace treaty between General Howard and Cochise. He also accused Geronimo of breaking his promise to come to San Carlos the year before. Now, he said, he had come to bring him in.

His eyes flashing with anger, Geronimo answered defiantly, "We are not going to San Carlos with you. And unless you are very careful, you and your Apache police will not go back to San Carlos either. Your bodies will stay here at Warm Springs to make food for Coyotes."

At that moment, Clum wished that he had waited for the army reinforcements. He and his chief of police were the only white men for miles. But he had no time to think about that. He gave a secret signal. The doors of

Reservation agent John Clum (in foreground) and a contingent of his Apache police, pictured in 1876.

the abandoned building burst open and the rest of the police came out running, rifles in hand, and formed a half circle around the edge of the compound.

Some of the Apaches began to back away. Then one of the women ran forward and threw her arms around the neck of the police chief, pulling down his gun. There was a struggle, during which Clum watched Geronimo's finger creeping toward the trigger on his rifle. Then one of the police grabbed the woman, and the rest raised their guns and aimed them at the renegades. When he saw Geronimo's finger move back, Clum knew he had won. He was never to forget the look of intense hatred on Geronimo's face at that moment. It was the only time that Geronimo was ever captured, and like Mangas Coloradas, he had been tricked.

Clum had the prisoners taken to the blacksmith's shop, where iron shackles and chains were attached to their ankles. Then they were taken to the guardhouse and given food, blankets, and beds of hay. The police stood guard while the Apache women and children returned to their camp to collect their belongings. Soon after, the cavalry arrived with orders that Clum was to bring not only Geronimo, but all the Warm Springs Apaches to San Carlos. Clum sent Victorio to round up his people for counting.

In May, Clum began the 400-mile march back to San Carlos. There were 450 Indians in the party, and although Clum wrote that they were a "happy, hopeful" group, many of the Apaches themselves later recorded that it was an agonizing trip. There was a lot of bad feeling among the Indians. Many of the Warm Springs Apaches blamed the renegades for getting them in trouble and causing them to lose their homeland. Four babies were born en route, and the new mothers rode in the wagon with the prisoners in irons. Then, one of the warriors

Victorio, a prominent leader of the Warm Springs band, loved his homeland. When allowed to remain there, he kept the peace; any attempt to relocate him brought war.

caught smallpox. Soon others were infected. In all, eight Apaches died of the disease before they reached San Carlos.

As far as Clum was concerned, his first order of business when he got back to the reservation was to send his prisoners to Tucson for trial, and then to see that they were hanged. But another matter would force him to delay: On his return, he found a company of soldiers camped outside his headquarters with orders to inspect and manage the Indians. Clum was furious. He was a proud, confident man who did not appreciate having his authority challenged.

Clum put Geronimo and the other prisoners in the San Carlos guardhouse and told the rest of the Indians they were free to make their camps anywhere on the reservation. Then he informed the company's commanding officer that he was in charge, and sent a telegram to the commissioner of Indian affairs in Washington, asking him to remove the troops. In the end, Clum's request was denied, and he resigned in a huff.

Geronimo later wrote that he was told there had been a trial, though he had not been present, and then he was released. But his arrest had a profound effect on him. His months spent in irons were a frightening, humiliating experience, and he knew well that he had come very close to being killed.

Clum stayed in Arizona Territory for the rest of his life and later became mayor of Tombstone (a wild town that was famous for its gunfights) and founder of the *Tombstone Epitaph* newspaper. For many years he wrote in his paper that not hanging Geronimo while the army had the chance was the worst mistake the U.S. military had ever made.

The agents who replaced Clum at San Carlos were mostly corrupt, like the agents before him. Many of the Warm Springs band were starving, poorly clothed, and in need of medical attention for smallpox and malaria, which they caught from the mosquitoes on the reservation. They watched as their rations were sold to others. Then, more land was taken from them. Prospectors, who were never prevented from crossing reservation boundaries, discovered a new silver deposit and convinced the authorities to give them the land.

Finally, late in the summer of 1877, Victorio, Loco, and Nana planned to break out. Careful not to be seen by the soldiers, or by the Apache spies sent among them by the agent, they began to save food and supplies. On September 1, they escaped into the mountains, taking 323 Warm Springs men, women, and children, and leaving behind 143 members of their band, including some of their relatives. For the time being, Geronimo, and most of the Chiricahua Apaches, now led by Naiche (Taza had died of pneumonia), elected to stay at San Carlos.

The fugitives went directly to Fort Wingate in Navajo country in New Mexico Territory, where they offered to come in and live peacefully, but they were turned away. While officials in Washington debated over what to do with the homeless Warm Springs band, they were allowed to drift back to their former reservation, where they remained for the winter. Hoping that by some chance they might be allowed to stay, they were very careful to keep the peace—and there was not one report of trouble with settlers or travelers in the area.

Meanwhile, back at San Carlos, conditions had not improved. Geronimo was now leading the remaining Warm Springs Indians. The agent made him promise to stay on the reservation, but as he grew more dissatisfied, he began to steal guns and ammunition, in preparation for a breakout. Then one night, when Geronimo was drinking tiswin, he scolded his nephew—the son of Nana and one of his sisters—seemingly for no reason. He was immediately sorry, but unfortunately the boy was deeply hurt. Normally, Apaches scolded children only when they did something very wrong. Geronimo's nephew had also been drinking. Later he got depressed and committed suicide.

Geronimo blamed himself for the boy's death, but he was also fed up with the situation his people were in, which he felt contributed to the horrible incident. Geronimo found it impossible to stay on the reservation any longer. After a few days, he gathered those who wanted to go and left. Soon, he met up with Juh and a group of Nednais in Mexico. Together they attacked a wagon train, killing the drivers and taking the food and ammunition.

Naiche, one of Cochise's sons, photographed by A. Frank Randall in 1884. Naiche took over the official leadership of the Chiricahuas after his brother Taza, who had been the designated leader, died of pneumonia.

Around this time, the summer of 1878, the BIA ordered the army to remove the Warm Springs Apaches from their homeland once again and take them back to San Carlos. When they saw the army coming, the band fled, but after a long chase the army captured about half of them—20 warriors, including Loco, and about 150 women and children. Victorio, Nana, and the rest of the warriors escaped. Victorio had tried repeatedly to make peace with the Americans. All he asked was that he be allowed to stay on a small part of his homeland. When he was forced to leave it for the last time, his anger grew so fierce that he seemed to care about nothing but causing the Americans as much pain as possible. With Nana, he began one of the bloodiest killing sprees in the history of the Apache wars. Demonstrating none of the usual Apache caution, they attacked ranches, wagon trains, and even small towns, stealing everything they could, and killing everyone they met. The attacks lasted more than a year. But Victorio and Nana were greatly outnumbered and finally their luck began to change.

In October 1880, the Mexican military laid a trap for the outlaw band, which had crossed the border into Mexico. Everything was over in a few minutes. The Mexican force appeared from behind rocks and trees and quickly killed 78 Indians, including Victorio himself, and captured 68 women and children to sell as slaves. Only 17 members of the band escaped the massacre, including Nana, who began another series of attacks. Eventually the military gave up and abandoned the chase.

Victorio and Nana had been causing such an enormous uproar that the pressure from the military soon started to affect Geronimo and Juh as well. It became more and more hazardous to raid, and Geronimo decided that for the time being he would rather return to the reservation and live quietly. In a meeting in which Thomas Jeffords once again served as interpreter, he surrendered to General Orlando Willcox. By the time Victorio was killed in Mexico, Geronimo was back at San Carlos.

When Geronimo returned to the reservation, there was a new agent in charge, Joseph Tiffany—a man who would go down in history as the most corrupt agent of all. Later, investigators sent from Washington found that Tiffany had not only sold rations that were supposed to go to the Indians but had built himself a ranch where he raised government-issued cattle, fed them government-issued grain, and then ordered an Apache warrior to take care of his herd.

The Indians on the reservation were demoralized. They had lost their families, their land, and their whole way of life. When they had surrendered and tried to please the Americans, they were treated with disrespect and denied the rations they were promised. Into this sorry atmosphere came a White Mountain Apache named Noch-ay-del-klinne. He claimed to be a religious prophet who could communicate with dead Apaches and even bring their lost chiefs back to life. Before long, he had many followers. They went to him every day to ask for advice, to pray, and to perform a feverish new dance he had taught them.

Geronimo was not as easily influenced by the prophet as some of the others who believed in him because he brought hope back to their life. Remaining skeptical, Geronimo visited Noch-ay-del-klinne's dwelling in a remote part of the reservation. Later he decided that the prophet might have Power, but he doubted that any man could bring dead Apaches back to life.

The authorities at San Carlos did not consider this new "ghost" religion as harmless as Geronimo did. The dancing reminded them of what they had heard of Apache war dances, and they feared that Noch-ay-del-klinne would soon lead an enormous uprising. Agent

Becoming increasingly concerned that he would be arrested at any moment by soldiers on the reservation, Geronimo escaped once again.

Tiffany sent his Indian police to investigate the matter, and they too became followers of the new religion. This frightened Tiffany even more. Next he told his men he wanted Noch-ay-del-klinne "arrested or killed or both."

The prophet surrendered peacefully when the soldiers arrived, but his devoted followers would not let him be taken so easily. There was a fight and many people, including Noch-ay-del-klinne, were killed. The incident created quite a stir among the residents of Arizona Territory who still feared that the Indians were about to revolt, and soon military reinforcements were brought in from New Mexico Territory and California. Whereas there had been relatively few military men on the reservation before, now hundreds of armed soldiers marched over every corner in an effort to prevent the expected uprising.

Naturally, this made Geronimo nervous. He was not sure whether the authorities knew of the things he had done during his latest visit to Mexico. As time went on, he expected to be arrested any day. Finally, when he could stand it no longer, he went to Tiffany and asked why the soldiers had come. He reminded the agent that he had surrendered in good faith and was now living a quiet, peaceful life. The agent assured him that the soldiers were not there to arrest him. Geronimo went back to his camp feeling very much relieved.

Then one night, a group of soldiers came to where Geronimo was camped and arrested a warrior who had been involved in the battle over the prophet. Even though the soldiers did not bother Geronimo, he saw this as a bad omen. Most of the Apaches were upset at having so many soldiers around, and some felt that the only way they could protect themselves was to leave. In early October 1881, 74 warriors under Geronimo, Juh, and the formerly peaceful Naiche left San Carlos with their families and headed for Mexico.

The Sierra Madre provided excellent hideouts for the Apaches. They used the mountain range's concealed recesses and tortuous passages to elude the Mexicans and the Americans who were pursuing them.

6

OUTLAW BANDS UNITE

Geronimo and the other outlaws decided that they would be safer in Mexico than on the American side of the border, where there were more large settlements. Geronimo knew the military would be after them in either country. But whereas the Americans had a seemingly endless supply of soldiers and weapons, the Mexican army was less well equipped. Mexico offered the outlaws another advantage as well. Even more than the mountains in Arizona and New Mexico territories, the Sierra Madre was full of concealed canyons, caves, and unexpected rock formations that came together in complicated ways, creating mazes where the Apaches could hide.

Although he knew breaking out put him and his people at enormous risk, Geronimo soon found himself feeling happier than he had been in a long time. As the group made its way silently through the countryside at night and hid during the day, he felt a sense of freedom and adventure that reminded him of his years as a young warrior. Being arrested had forced Geronimo to try reservation life, but now he realized that even if conditions had not been so intolerable, passivity did not suit him. Within a few days of leaving San Carlos, he began to feel his old strength return, and with it his hatred for the Americans and the Mexicans who were his enemies.

Geronimo led the band in a blaze of raiding and killing through southern Arizona Territory. No one who got close to them was allowed to live. The army attempted two attacks, but neither was successful.

Several months later, the outlaws reached Mexico. They had accumulated large quantities of stolen food and blankets, as well as horses for all the warriors and more rifles so that every man was armed. Their first stop was the base of a tall mountain where Nana and his band of Warm Springs Apaches were hiding.

For a few days, the combined bands held councils to decide what they would do next. Geronimo's excitement was contagious. Soon the entire group longed to return to their traditional ways. Using cloth they had stolen after the breakout, the women made new breechcloths for the warriors, which they donned for a war dance. For the first time in many years, the chanting of Apaches echoed through the canyon and up into the sky.

Geronimo (center) and his renegade warriors, pictured in 1886. Much of Geronimo's influence over his people stemmed from his abilities as a shaman, or medicine man.

With Geronimo now leading the group, the decision was made to send a party back to San Carlos to rescue their friends and relatives, now led by Loco. Geronimo knew that the Apaches at San Carlos would soon be facing the hot summer months, when malaria was most widespread, cheated of their rations and with no means of self-support. The additional reinforcements would also add to the outlaws' strength.

It was decided that Geronimo and Naiche would lead a group of about 60 warriors to San Carlos to get Loco and the others. Juh would continue to raid to maintain their supply of food and ammunition. Nana would stay behind to protect the women and children.

Geronimo led his men back to the border, occasionally stopping to raid when an opportunity presented itself. Most of the band had no trouble, though the Apaches saw many Mexican forces along the well-worn trail. Two of Geronimo's warriors were not so lucky, however. They were caught stealing horses from a Mexican peasant they found on the road. In exchange for their lives, the two warriors told the Mexican officers about Geronimo's plan to rescue the other Apaches at San Carlos. Feeling confident at last that they would catch the great Geronimo, the Mexicans planned to trap him on his return journey.

By this time, Geronimo's abilities as a war shaman were believed to be an important asset to the band. The day before they arrived at the reservation, he left the others as they made camp and went alone into a small patch of trees to consult his Power about his return to San Carlos. He sang four songs, and then his Power spoke to him, saying that the mission would be successful. Geronimo also asked his Power to make sure the police at the reservation would be in a deep sleep the following night.

At dusk, the band prepared to travel the last distance to San Carlos, this time in small groups so that they would less likely be seen in the populated areas. They arranged to meet again in a clearing beside the Gila River across from the east boundary of the reservation. When they arrived, Geronimo sent three warriors to determine the position of the police and to cut the telegraph wires connecting the reservation headquarters to an outpost near the Apache camp. Then, at daybreak, they crossed the river. It was April 19, 1882.

The Indians on the reservation awoke to shouting and saw a row of armed warriors around their camp. More were swimming their horses across the river. When he found Loco, Geronimo told him that he had come to take them back to Mexico. To Geronimo's surprise, Loco did not want to go. He argued that although their living conditions were bad, they at least were at peace. This was a blow for Geronimo, but he had not come several hundred miles to go back empty-handed. Thinking that Loco would feel different when he was free, as he himself had, Geronimo forced him to tell the others to gather their belongings and to lead them out. The commotion woke two of the police, who were quickly shot.

Seeing the police killed convinced Loco's people that it was senseless to oppose Geronimo's plan. Later, one of them named Jason Betinez wrote in his book *I Fought with Geronimo*, "We did everything they told us to do. We knew that our safety depended on keeping quiet and not trying to escape."

Filled with despair, the newly "rescued" Apaches were herded along the river for several miles until they were too tired to continue. Geronimo allowed them to rest while some of the warriors went out to raid. They soon returned with a herd of sheep to eat. There were now nearly 400 in the group—about 100 warriors and 300 women and children.

Most of the people in the band had lived on a reservation for so long that they were not up to traveling with the usual Apache speed and endurance. Many of the young men had received little training as warriors, and having grown up at San Carlos, they did not even have experience as hunters. As he walked among the miserable group, Geronimo began to feel that he had made a mistake. These poor people would be helpless against enemy forces.

More warriors were sent to steal supplies and horses for the captives. Another day was spent breaking the horses and making improvised saddles from bundles of reeds. By the time the Apaches were ready to resume traveling, Geronimo's men had killed 50 people in the surrounding countryside. This destroyed any possibility of the reservation Indians returning untainted by crimes. Though many still wanted to turn back, Loco resigned himself to whatever lay ahead and was invited by Geronimo to join the council of warriors.

Geronimo kept the large group marching through several long nights. Those who resisted were surrounded as they rode. As they crossed the wide San Simon Valley in southern Arizona Territory, Geronimo called on his Power to "hold back the morning" for two or three hours until they could reach the protection of the mountains in Mexico. During the trip, Geronimo sent scouts into the countryside. They saw several companies of soldiers, led by Lieutenant Colonel George Forsyth, pursuing them. But Forsyth did not attack, and the Apaches crossed the border into Mexico unharmed.

Having eluded the American forces, Geronimo believed his people were safe, for he had little respect for the fighting abilities of the Mexicans. He encouraged the Indians to celebrate their newfound freedom. For many of the Apaches who had not left San Carlos for years, it was truly a magnificent experience. They rode under the

stars singing, laughing, and challenging each other to short races on their new horses. Then Geronimo allowed them to stop and rest in a canyon near a spring. While they were there, Forsyth attacked. Fourteen warriors were killed, and many of the women and children were wounded. The rest of the Indians disappeared into the mountains.

Moving slowly to accommodate the wounded, Geronimo led his frightened charges deeper into Mexico,

Apache women and children at Turkey Creek on San Carlos reservation, late 19th century. Although much of this reservation was unsuitable for farming, U.S. officials were determined to turn the Indians into farmers.

where he planned to rendezvous with Nana and Juh. The band had escaped with almost nothing. Their horses were gone, as were most of the supplies, such as the blankets and utensils they had brought from San Carlos. The little food they had was distributed among them as they stumbled on foot through the night, but it was not nearly enough. Soon they were hungry, cold, and utterly exhausted.

Stopping for only an hour or so to rest and see to the wounded, they had traveled nearly 29 miles by dawn, much of it across the Janos Plains, a relatively flat area. Though Geronimo tried to keep them together, the slowest were nearly two miles behind as the band marched in a long, straggling line. A few warriors who had horses were assigned to guard the rear of the line and watch for pursuing soldiers. Forsyth did not attack again, but Mexican forces under Colonel Lorenzo Garcia did. He had been alerted to the Apaches' plans by the two warriors who were with Geronimo's party and were caught stealing horses while the band was on its way to San Carlos. Struck from the side, the long line of tired, wounded Apaches was devastated. Betinez described the scene:

> Almost immediately Mexicans were right among us all, shooting down women and children right and left. People were falling and bleeding, and dying, on all sides of us. . . . Those who could run the fastest and the farthest managed to escape. . . . My mother and sister and I were among them, being excellent runners. . . . I had no weapons of any kind. We headed rapidly for the mountains. As we ran, my mother and I heard Geronimo behind us, calling to the men to gather around him and make a stand to protect the women and children. We learned later that thirty-two warriors responded to Geronimo, around whom some women and children assembled for protection.

As the Mexicans fired on the fleeing Apaches, Geronimo and a few warriors and some women and children made a stand in a dry creek bed. The women dug holes in the side of the ravine to provide shelter and footholds for the men as they stepped up to shoot over the edge. While they were digging they also found water to drink. When they were nearly out of ammunition, one brave woman ran out in a hail of gunfire and grabbed a bag of bullets that had been left a few yards away.

The battle continued until dark. Then somebody set the grass on fire. Later, the Mexicans said they did it to smoke out the Indians, and the Apaches said they did it to provide cover for them to get away. In the confusion, Geronimo and his people escaped to join those who had fled to the mountains. From there he could see the carnage on the field and counted 22 dead Mexican soldiers and 78 Indians (of which only 11 were warriors).

On the mountainside, the Apaches wailed softly, grieving for their dead relatives. Because it was not safe to build fires, they covered themselves with grass for protection from the cold. There was no help for the wounded and no food. Soon after, Geronimo moved them through the successive mountain ranges. The warriors began the old task of raiding for food and supplies, and before long they brought back a small herd of cattle— providing the first meal the Indians had had since Forsyth attacked their camp three days earlier.

When they resumed their journey two days later, a warrior named Tsoe, whose brother had been killed in the battle, began to cry and told Geronimo that he could not go on. Geronimo gave him some supplies and wished him well. Tsoe set off alone, hoping to return to the reservation.

In time the surviving Apaches reached their base camp in the Sierra Madre and were reunited with Nana and

Tsoe was considered a traitor by the Apaches. Sometime after leaving Geronimo's band, he led the U.S. military to the renegades' hideout in the Sierra Madre. Tsoe was nicknamed Peaches by the soldiers on account of his smooth, fair complexion.

Juh and the rest of their band. Geronimo was greeted with some shocking news. During the separation, Juh's group had also been attacked. Geronimo's favorite cousin, Ishton, and her young daughter had been killed.

The past days' events had inflamed Geronimo's rage, and he spent every moment dreaming of the ruthless revenge he would inflict on both the Mexicans and the Americans. He waited impatiently for the others to recuperate and then began to make new plans. Even though they suffered great losses, the combined bands represented the largest group of Apaches assembled in many years.

Relying on his intuition, as he often did in military matters, Geronimo sensed that it was time for the band to move to a new campsite, one that would offer the large group maximum protection. He took them west to a place that was later called simply the Great Canyon. It was a beautiful spot, with plenty of fresh water, firewood, and game for hunting. But more important, it had nearly vertical walls well over 1,000 feet high that made it virtually impregnable. No American or Mexican had ever laid eyes on this canyon, and Geronimo used it as his headquarters from which to raid. Soon he had the band fully armed again and ready for war.

In the months that followed, Geronimo led the largest group that would ever be under his command. Rekindling his days as a young warrior, he planned attacks on villages to avenge the recent deaths suffered by the band. Then he watched with satisfaction as his plans were carried out with faultless precision by his warriors.

For Geronimo it was an almost idyllic time. There was plenty of excitement, but not too much danger. While he and his men went out in small groups to attack Mexican villages, driving off herds of cattle, horses, and mules and capturing pack trains, their families were safely hidden in the mountains. For their part, the women dried beef, gathered and stored wild herbs and berries, and made clothing out of the ever increasing supply of brightly colored cloth brought back by the men.

All was not perfect however. Though most of his raids were successful, Geronimo's wife Chee-hash-kish, mother of his teenage son and daughter, was captured by the Mexicans. Geronimo never saw her again. Sometime later he married a much younger Nednai woman named Zi-yeh, who would live with him through his old age.

Once again the outlaws had the entire region in an uproar. It seemed they could go anywhere, steal anything, kill at will—and not get caught. At this time, a federal judge, H. C. McComas, his wife, and his six-year-old son, Charlie, were traveling in a stagecoach through the territory and fell victim to an Apache attack. The adults were killed, and the boy was taken to live with the Indians. The death of these well-known people induced the military to bring back General Crook.

When Crook arrived he inspected the reservations and learned that the Indians there had indeed been cheated and virtually "scared away" by the influx of the military. He fired the current agent and replaced him with a more honorable one. Then someone introduced him to Tsoe, the Indian who had left Geronimo's band. Considering Geronimo responsible for the deaths among the people he forced to leave San Carlos, Tsoe agreed to help Crook find Geronimo's hideout.

After obtaining permission from the Mexican government, Crook led his men into the formidable mountains of Mexico. With the knowledgeable Tsoe as their guide, they threaded through a jungle of canyons and made many hazardous climbs up mountains where all except the Apache scouts among them could hardly hold on. As they got closer to the outlaws' hideout in the Great Canyon, Crook's men began to see signs of Apache life:

Six-year-old Charlie Mc-Comas was kidnapped by the Apaches after they killed his parents. Because these people were well known, their death spurred on the military in its pursuit of Geronimo.

abandoned camps dotted with the frames of dismantled wickiups, ashes from fires, straw beds, a play area, and stones for grinding acorn meal.

Many miles away, Geronimo was sitting with a few warriors eating a piece of meat when he stopped suddenly. He had a vision that his sanctuary had been invaded by white men. Although they had planned to attack a settlement the following day, Geronimo ordered his men to pack up and return to the Great Canyon. Many hours later the group approached the canyon. From atop a nearby mountain Geronimo could see that Crook had indeed come, just as he had pictured.

Crook had been in the canyon for several days, and by the time Geronimo got there, the general had convinced many of the Indians to go back with him. The life of a hunted Apache was difficult. Many of the Indians Geronimo brought from the reservation never fully adapted to the rough life and were relieved to give it up. Others were sorry to lose their freedom.

Geronimo and his small band made camp on the mountain. From there many messages were sent back and forth between him and Crook before he too agreed to surrender. Geronimo made a long speech in which he told Crook in detail of the bad way the Apaches had been treated at San Carlos. Crook had seen the evidence himself and assured Geronimo that he had corrected the situation.

Geronimo then asked Crook to wait for him to gather the rest of his people who were still spread out among the mountains. With so many Indians now under his protection, Crook felt it was unwise to wait. For one thing, he did not have enough food. He also knew that the Indians would not be safe from the Mexicans once they were found. Crook warned Geronimo that if he came in alone, he would once again face the risk of being attacked by Mexicans and by angry American citizens. Then, the general left.

7

SURRENDER OR FIGHT

The balance of trust between Geronimo and the U.S. military was always much more complicated than it appeared. Like Agent Clum, many of the officers who knew Geronimo considered him a liar. But, from another point of view, Geronimo had never made a serious promise he did not keep. Years earlier, when he broke away from Agent Clum at the Chiricahua reservation, he had not made a promise to stay, and so he felt he owed Clum nothing. But when he surrendered to General Crook, Geronimo looked the general in the eye, shook his hand, and gave his solemn word that he would return to the San Carlos reservation. These actions may have appeared insignificant to some non-Indians, but Crook understood the Apaches better than most. He knew that Geronimo fully intended to return to the reservation, and when the Apache leader and his people did not appear after several months, the general was only mildly worried. Despite pressure from his superiors in Washington and from civilian groups who feared that Geronimo would attack at any moment, he wrote in his report that even though Geronimo was still at large, it was "of no significance." Geronimo's actions would prove that Crook's assessment of the situation was basically correct.

The Apache leader began gathering his people from the Mexican mountains in preparation for their return to

At a San Antonio prison in the 1880s, Geronimo waits while U.S. officials debate his fate. He fully expected to be executed.

91

San Carlos. Around this time, he got word that Juh had died of a heart attack while trading outside a Mexican town. Juh's son Daklugie was with him at the time, and Geronimo took over the training of his "nephew." Geronimo continued to make preparations for returning to San Carlos, but in his usual independent manner, he did not see any reason to hurry. He was more than 60 years old when he promised Crook that he would give up his freedom and spend the rest of his years on the reservation. In spite of Crook's assurances that there would be no more dishonest agents at San Carlos, Geronimo knew from previous experience that the word of one U.S. officer was often disregarded after that officer was replaced. He was concerned that if the pleasant situation Crook described should change, he might be too old to support himself and his family in the years to come.

With these thoughts in mind, Geronimo continued to raid in Mexico until he had assembled a herd of more than 350 cattle. He planned to establish a ranch on the reservation where he would breed the animals and sell them. The venture would give him security in his old age and an ongoing source of food if the Indians were denied their rations as they had been in the past. In February of 1884, approximately eight months after Crook left him behind, Geronimo began the journey north to San Carlos.

At the American border he was met by Second Lieutenant Britton Davis, who had been sent by Crook with two companies of Indian scouts to guard the Apaches on their way through American territory. Geronimo returned peacefully but insisted that the group travel slowly so that his cattle would arrive at the reservation in good health.

A couple of weeks after returning to San Carlos, Geronimo made a formal statement of his position to

General George Crook promised Geronimo that there would be no more dishonest agents on the reservation. But Geronimo knew that the general's word was no guarantee that other officials would abide by his promise.

Captain Emmet Crawford, who was in charge of the reservation at the time, and asked him to forward it to General Crook. The statement covered a number of issues that were important to the Apaches, and Geronimo made every effort to present it in a way that would convince the general to give him what he wanted. He had been careful to obtain the full support of his people before speaking, and each concern was expressed clearly, with careful consideration given to the practicality of his requests. The statement is a precise indication of Geronimo's character in his later years. It shows his capacity for logical thinking, his good economic sense, his feeling of responsibility for the others, and his talent for diplomacy when dealing with American authorities. Crawford took notes as Geronimo talked. It was a long session (also typical of Geronimo). When it was over the military had an official record of the Apache leader's thoughts and feelings at the time. Crawford recorded that Geronimo wanted the past forgotten.

> He wants everything to be done straight. All made new, so that they can begin again. Before, here in San Carlos, everything was wrong with the Indians. But now it is all being carried on straight, and he wants it to continue. He will never think again as he used to think before; now he thinks, that the Americans on the reservation want him to live here, and have cooking utensils, etc. and not run around in the mountains cooking his meat on sticks before the fire.

Geronimo followed this by explaining that it would not be easy for his people to take up "civilized" pursuits, and Crawford recorded his words. "[He says] they are all here now like bronco mules, which it is necessary to teach little by little, until they are all tamed. . . . He feels now as if he were in a big hole and covered up as far as his chest. . . . He has surrendered entirely, and any orders given him he will obey without thinking of resisting them."

Geronimo was most concerned with finding a good place for his people to live. He did not see why they should be confined within the reservation boundaries. The piece of land Geronimo wanted was the land surrounding Eagle Creek, a valley that had been a part of the original agreement made with General Howard before Cochise died. Crawford went on to record: "[Geronimo says] there is plenty of land, plenty of grass and his people can all live there together. Those Americans who live on Eagle Creek, can't their land be bought from them and given to the Indians? [The Indians] take great interest in good land, as they want to farm and live like white men, and think that Eagle Creek would be good for them. . . . All of them have the same things as white men, hands, legs, arms, etc. and Geronimo is surprised that they are not given the same things as white men when they ask for them. This peace they promised was a legal peace and they expect to get the land they want on account of having made this peace."

Geronimo did not get the land at Eagle Creek, and that was not his only disappointment. Soon after the statement was made, Crook was forced to take Geronimo's cattle away from him. He overlooked the fact that all the horses Geronimo's people were riding when they came in had been stolen from the Mexicans, but he could not justify allowing them to keep such a large herd of stolen cattle. Eventually the cattle were sold and the proceeds were turned over to the Mexican government. Of course, Geronimo was outraged at this after working so hard to collect the herd.

Crook told Geronimo that he and his band could settle anywhere on the reservation they wished. They chose Turkey Creek, which offered clear running water and a small forest of pine trees, but it lacked good farmland. Most of the best reservation land was already taken by other tribes.

Geronimo's idea of raising cattle would have made the most sense because Turkey Creek was highly suitable for such a purpose. Other tribes had already established farms, and the army had been buying corn and barley from these Indians for some time. U.S. officials were determined that all the Indians would learn farming. Before the Apaches were moved to Turkey Creek, Crawford ordered picks, shovels, seed, a dozen light wagons, and a dozen plows for them. Lieutenant Davis was given the job of training Geronimo and the others to use the equipment. Later he wrote that it was a hilarious experience, with the Indians yelling and laughing as their horses pulled the plows at a gallop so that the plowman in back could barely hold on and the plow hardly touched the soil.

In late May, Davis set out for Turkey Creek with the entire band—a total of 521, including 127 men and boys old enough to use a rifle. Davis would be in charge of the settlement. He set up his tent under a pine tree, with a larger tent nearby where the rations were stored. Naiche and Geronimo, probably still upset over his cattle, made camp several miles away from Davis, as did some of the other less-trusting Apaches. Loco and Mangus, son of Mangas Coloradas, made their homes closer to the lieutenant. Many of them liked Davis and went to his tent often to talk business or just to visit. Even Geronimo's son Chappo took a job as Davis's striker, or paid servant.

Davis treated the Indians well for the most part, but some of his policies, such as using spies to obtain information about the Apaches, encouraged distrust within the band. In addition, Geronimo and some of the other leaders were upset that he did not allow them to

Second Lieutenant Britton Davis was assigned the task of training Geronimo's people to use farm equipment. Most of the Indians liked Davis because he treated them well.

make tiswin. One day they came to his tent to discuss the matter. They argued that they had promised Crook to keep the peace and were holding to their part of the bargain, but the banning of tiswin had not been mentioned in their negotiations. Although drinking the alcoholic beverage often led to fights, they reasoned that since "all the white men" drank something to "make them feel good" it was unfair to deny this right to the Indians.

The other rule Apache men were finding very hard to live with was the ban on physical abuse of their wives. For hundreds of years, Apache men and women alike upheld a tradition whereby a husband cut off the tip of his wife's nose if he found her to be unfaithful, thus leaving her with a shameful scar. Since Crook had forbidden this, men had resorted to beating women in these situations. A man who took no action at all lost the respect of others in the band. In some cases, Apache warriors had even killed their unfaithful wives and then killed themselves, rather than bear such humiliation. Davis listened to what Geronimo and the others had to say, but on orders from Crook, he stood firm on these issues.

Not long after this meeting, Davis was awakened one night by one of his spies, who said that Geronimo and Kaahteney, a warrior with some followers of his own, were planning an uprising. Davis confronted the Indians and arrested Kaahteney. Geronimo denied playing any part in the scheme. Kaahteney had been dissatisfied for a long time, and Davis thought it would be best for the whole band if he were sent away. He was taken to Alcatraz, an island prison off the coast of San Francisco, California.

The Indians at Turkey Creek lived for about a year with no other mishaps. Davis even reported that

Cut-Nosed Woman, photo-graphed by A. Frank Randall in 1884. One Apache tradition, forbidden by reservation offi-cials, held that a man must cut off the end of his wife's nose if she was unfaithful.

Geronimo was one of the best farmers in the group. Nevertheless, unknown to Davis, Geronimo and the other leaders were becoming increasingly suspicious. Because Kaahteney had been arrested without actually doing anything, it seemed perfectly plausible to the other leaders that Davis's spies might make up a story and get them arrested too. To make matters worse, some of the soldiers found it amusing to frighten the Indians by making the sign of death by drawing their hand across their throat. Though Davis claimed to know nothing of this, he did notice that Geronimo began to need almost constant reassurances that he would not be arrested, that Crook had not left them for good, and that Kaahteney was not dead.

Then one night a group of about 30 armed warriors led by Geronimo came to Davis's camp. It was clear that many of them had been drinking, even Loco, who had always been one of the most cooperative in the group. They said they had come to talk and began crowding into the lieutenant's small tent. Knowing that the situation could explode at any moment, Davis tried to explain Crook's reasons for the rules that were upsetting them.

To avoid a possible confrontation, Davis told the group that the matter was too serious for him to decide alone but that he would send a telegram to Crook. As it turned out, the telegraph machine was broken. Day after day went by with no word while both the Indians and Davis waited anxiously. Then one afternoon, one of Davis's spies came to him and reported that a group of Apaches led by Geronimo, Naiche, Mangus, and Nana had left the reservation. He called in the remaining Indians to be counted and found that 35 men and 109 women and children—one-quarter of the band—had broken out.

Before long every newspaper in the Southwest screamed the headline THE APACHES ARE OUT! Settlers and travelers hurried to army bases for safety, but many were too late. Believing that they were running for their life, Geronimo and the others killed everyone they came across, stealing as they went. A large military contingent set out in pursuit. Knowing that the Indians would most likely head for Mexico, Crook stationed troops at all the key places on the American side of the border, and then ordered 200 Indian scouts to trail the outlaws. In one battle, many of the women and children were captured, including Geronimo's wives Zi-yeh and She-gha. In Apache culture, a warrior without a woman to cook and make clothes for him was seriously handicapped. To remedy this, Geronimo and the others slipped back to the reservation to "steal wives," a common practice in these situations. Geronimo recovered She-gha and his three-year-old daughter and also took a Mescalero Apache woman named Ih.-tedda or "young one." Closely pursued by the soldiers, the band continued to avoid capture for several months.

Finally, in March 1886, two of the scouts under Captain Crawford reported that they had found the outlaws' camp in Mexico. Geronimo and Naiche sent word to Crawford that they wished to hold a conference with General Crook.

It took Crook almost a week to reach Geronimo's position in the Cañón de los Embudos in Mexico. Their conference was held on the afternoon of March 25, 1886, under some large cottonwood and sycamore trees. The leaders sat in a circle with Crook while other armed warriors stood by, ready to shoot if there were any signs of trouble. As usual, Crook assigned one of his assistants to record every word that was said, so there could be no confusion later.

Crook knew that he could no longer offer Geronimo the option of returning peacefully to the reservation. Too much damage had been done. The military and the citizens of the Southwest had demanded that he be taken prisoner. Many were calling for his execution. This put Crook in a difficult position: If he refused to negotiate and demanded unconditional surrender as he had been ordered to, Geronimo would never agree to come in. At the same time, Crook had never lied to the Indians, and he had no intention of making false promises. In the end, he decided that rather than allow Geronimo to go on raiding and killing, he would try to get him to agree to the harshest terms possible, and deal with his superiors later.

The March 25, 1886, council between Geronimo's band of outlaws and General Crook (second from right, facing Geronimo) and his men. The band once more agreed to surrender and to spend two years in prison.

At first the Indians would only consider returning to the reservation, but finally a compromise was reached: All the warriors would be sent to prison in the East for not more than two years with any members of their families that wished to go with them, after which they would live out their life in peace on a reservation. One by one the leaders began to surrender. Geronimo was the last to hold out.

Crook went on ahead, leaving Lieutenant Marion P. Maus to follow with the Indians. After spending a sleepless night listening to shouting and gunshots coming from the Indians' camp, Maus received word that Geronimo and Naiche, with 20 men, 14 women, and 6 children had slipped into the mountains, taking only 2 horses and 1 mule.

When Crook reached Fort Bowie, he sent a telegram to Lieutenant General Philip H. Sheridan, commander in chief of the U.S. Army, and received an angry reply stating that Sheridan did not like the terms of the surrender and would not honor them. Then when he found out Geronimo had escaped yet again, Sheridan blamed Crook. Crook knew he had handled Geronimo better than any other officer could have, so he resigned. And on April 13, 1886, his replacement, Brigadier General Nelson A. Miles, arrived in Arizona Territory.

Miles was an experienced "Indian fighter," but he was always more interested in glory than in getting the job done. He knew little of the Apaches, and unlike Crook, he saw no reason to be honest with them. Miles brought in 5,000 U.S. troopers—one-quarter of the entire army at the time—to track down Geronimo and his small band. He did not like working with Indians, so he discharged the Apache scouts. Then he attempted to chase the Apaches with cavalry. When that failed, he had his men dismount and continue on foot, but he soon found that none of them was up to the hardships the Apaches endured every day.

Hunted and desperate, Geronimo attacked throughout Sonora and Arizona Territory and had no trouble evading Miles. In fact, the general's incompetence gave him the freedom to raid within a few miles of Fort Apache without losing a single warrior. But it was not like the old days. In his memoirs, Geronimo said, "We were reckless of our lives, because we felt that every man's hand was against us. If we returned to the reservation we would be put in prison and killed; if we stayed in Mexico they would continue to send soldiers to fight us; so we gave no quarter to anyone and asked no favors."

Then, after months of chasing the Indians without success, Miles turned his frustration against the nearly

400 Apaches living peacefully at San Carlos. By that time they had made a good start at farming, and even cut hay to sell at the post. Some of them had served the army as scouts, helping to track the outlaws. On July 3, 1886, Miles told Sheridan that he had inspected their camp and found them to be "turbulent and dissipated." His plan was to send them to Fort Sill, a reservation in present-day Oklahoma that was home to the Comanches and the Kiowas—two tribes that were long-time enemies of the Apaches of the Southwest. However, in 1879, the people in the states surrounding Fort Sill, especially Kansas, had persuaded Congress to pass an amendment to the Indian Appropriation Bill prohibiting Apaches or other Indians from New Mexico or Arizona territories to be placed there. Despite his position of authority, Miles was unable to get the amendment repealed. In the end, the BIA decided on Fort Marion in Florida, as the new "place of confinement" for the Apaches.

By keeping his plans for them secret, Miles was able to get two Apache warriors to help him take a message to Geronimo. He placed Lieutenant Charles Gatewood in charge of the mission and left to await the outcome at Fort Bowie. Gatewood took only one other soldier and an interpreter and left for the part of Mexico where Geronimo had recently been seen. When he reached the area, he sent the two Apaches to find the outlaw camp which they soon did.

Geronimo sent word agreeing to meet with Gatewood, who, when they came together, relayed the message from General Miles: surrender as a prisoner, or fight to the finish. At first, Geronimo and the others again insisted that they be allowed to return to the reservation, but Gatewood told them that the rest of their people were already in Florida, though in truth they had not yet left. This was a blow to Geronimo. He was silent for a long

Lieutenant Charles Gatewood, representing General Nelson Miles, convinced Geronimo to surrender. This was the fourth, and final, time the Apache leader would turn himself over to U.S. authorities.

time, and then he began to question Gatewood about General Miles. He was apparently very concerned about the general's trustworthiness. He asked Gatewood many questions—everything from how old Miles was to whether he had many friends. Then Geronimo asked the lieutenant what he would do if he were not a white man, but an Apache. Gatewood replied that he would accept Miles's offer. In the end, Geronimo opted for continuing the war, but in their councils the other warriors said they wanted to surrender. He eventually decided to go along with this decision. Gatewood took them to a post just over the border to wait for Miles.

When he arrived, Miles joked with Geronimo, called him his friend, and made many promises, such as "everything you have done up to this time will be wiped out . . . and forgotten, and you will begin a new life." "Leave your horses here," he said, "maybe they will be sent to you; you will have a separate reservation with your tribe, with horses and wagons, and no one will harm you." He described the prison in Florida as a beautiful place and promised the Indians that they would soon be reunited with their families. Then he made an impressive ceremony to seal the treaty by laying a stone on a blanket and vowing that the treaty would last until the stone crumbled to dust.

In his memoirs, written after 19 years as a prisoner of war, Geronimo said, "We did not believe Crook because he talked ugly, but Miles talked very friendly to us, and we believed him as we would God. . . . I looked in vain for General Miles to send me to that land of which he had spoken; I longed in vain for the implements, the house, and the stock that General Miles had promised me."

Geronimo spent several days in custody at Fort Bowie, and then he and the others were taken to a train at Bowie Station to begin their trip to Florida. On the way, Geronimo took a long look at the Chiricahua Mountains where he had spent much of his life. He turned to General Miles and said, "This is the fourth time I have surrendered." And Miles answered, "And I think it is the last time."

Geronimo and his band as prisoners of war, pictured on a railway embankment in San Antonio, Texas. In the front row, third from left is Naiche; Geronimo is fourth from left; and Chappo, one of Geronimo's sons, is fifth from left.

8

PRISONER OF WAR

On September 8, 1886, Geronimo and the other Apaches with him at the time of his surrender boarded the train at Bowie Station, in eastern Arizona Territory, bound for Florida. Trusting General Miles, they believed they would soon be reunited with the rest of their tribe. When word leaked out that Miles had made them this promise, there was an uproar in Washington. While General Sheridan and President Cleveland were deciding what to do, the train was stopped at San Antonio, Texas, where the prisoners waited.

Meanwhile, the larger group of Apaches was taken from San Carlos on September 13 and brought to the nearby Holbrook Station. They were being sent to Fort Marion, Florida, as the BIA had decided several months earlier. Most of the Indians had never seen a train before. As it came into the station, whistling and blowing smoke, many of the children ran into the woods in terror while some of the old men and women dropped to their knees to pray. Under guard, the Apaches were loaded into boxcars, and all the doors and windows were shut tight. Conditions on the train were so bad that even the guards, who had access to fresh air, got sick. The prisoners arrived at Fort Marion a week later. There were 381 in the band—278 adults and 103 children.

Finally, after eight days of deliberating, the president announced that in an effort to honor Miles's word, the outlaws' lives would be spared. But Miles's promise that they would be reunited with their tribe and someday given a reservation would be disregarded. On September 19, the secretary of war gave the following instructions:

> By direction of the President, it is ordered that the hostile Apache adult Indians be sent under proper guard to Fort Pickens, Florida, there to be kept in close custody until further orders. These Indians have been guilty of the worst crimes known to the law, committed under circumstances of great atrocity, and the public safety requires that they should be removed far from the scene of their depredations and guarded with the strictest vigilance.
>
> The remainder of the band, captured at the same time, you are to send to Fort Marion, and place with the other Apache Indians now under custody at that post.

On October 25, Geronimo and his small band of warriors were greeted by a crowd of tourists at Pensacola, Florida, before boarding a steamboat for Fort Pickens, which was located on Santa Rosa Island. One reporter wrote that Naiche seemed much amused by the people staring and pushing to get a glimpse of them. In fact, the ocean, the boat, the island with its white sand, and the dolphins playing in the waves, were all new experiences for the Apaches, and their guards said they were "delighted."

Fort Pickens had been abandoned since the Civil War, and although it was not in good repair, there was plenty of space. And the warriors led a relatively easy life, performing various manual chores five days a week and taking care of their own cleaning on weekends.

At Fort Marion, however, conditions were most unpleasant. The prison had been overcrowded even before the Apaches arrived. Now most of the newcomers were

Chappo Geronimo (left) and Jason Betinez as "civilized" Indians. They both attended Carlisle Indian School and were educated in the ways of Americans.

forced to sleep outside in the cement courtyard. The prison was also overrun by disease. There were 66 cases of illness in the first month. By the end of the year, 18 Apaches had died. In this atmosphere, Geronimo's Mescalero wife, Ih-tedda, gave birth to a daughter, who was given the name Lenna.

In an effort to alleviate the crowding and to speed up their assimilation, many of the older Apache children at Fort Marion were sent to the Carlisle Indian School in Pennsylvania. This was devastating for their parents, who grieved and even tried to hide them. Jason Betinez, Geronimo's son Chappo, and Daklugie all attended Carlisle. Founded in 1879, the school was designed to give the Indians a "white education." Their hair was cut and they were dressed in uniforms. Some of the students later graduated able to read and write English, but many others died there. Apparently, the school's first students were infected with tuberculosis, and a large percentage of those who followed also caught the disease.

While at Fort Pickens, Geronimo and the others were model prisoners. They cooperated completely with the authorities, but Geronimo sometimes became a nuisance to the guards with his repeated appeals to be reunited with his family. Finally, after several months, the families of the prisoners were allowed to join them, and Geronimo met his daughter Lenna for the first time. Also during this time, a young woman in the group reached maturity, and the prisoners were allowed to give her a womanhood ceremony. Tickets were sold to 300 spectators who apparently thought they were watching a Corn Dance designed to keep evil spirits from damaging the crop, a practice that had nothing to do with the Apaches.

In May 1888, the War Department decided to remove all the Apaches from Florida and send them to Mount Vernon Barracks in Alabama. They would live there as prisoners for seven years. When they arrived, there were many happy reunions. But as the post doctor soon discovered, a majority of the tribe was in poor health, suffering from a variety of illnesses—from pneumonia to meningitis. Soon, they would also suffer from semi-starvation. Six months after their arrival, a report written by commanding officer Major William Sinclair stated that the Indians were trying to sell their blankets and other private articles for food. Only after this report was filed did the army give them their full rations.

When they first arrived at Mount Vernon, the prisoners lived in tents. Then they were directed to build themselves log cabins from the trees surrounding the post, which they did in less than two months. They had no furniture and slept on the ground. Still, anything was better than the conditions at Fort Marion.

Soon, various philanthropic groups began to take an interest in helping the Apaches, who they found to be "a keen and intelligent people." Even General Crook assisted in convincing the president that they should be given a missionary school, and in February 1889, two teachers arrived. In a one-room building, they instructed about 80 of the children, including Geronimo's son Fenton, in English, geography, and other subjects.

Geronimo was a big supporter of the school. He realized that learning the ways of the whites would give the Apache children the best chance of a secure future. He gathered the children in the morning and stayed with them later as they did their schoolwork. He was also known to police the classroom with a stick in his hand to intimidate anyone who might misbehave. It was his way of perpetuating the Apache discipline he himself had experienced as a child.

In April 1889, General Howard, who was then in command of the Atlantic Division of the army, came to inspect the prisoners at Mount Vernon. Remembering their days in Cochise's mountain hideout and the peace that followed, Geronimo ran and threw his arms around the general. With the help of an interpreter, he began to tell Howard about the school. "We have fine lady teachers," Geronimo said. "All the children go to their school. I make them. I want them to be white children."

But the missionary school could only do so much. The

Apaches continued to die. Nine of the young people who had been sent to school at Carlisle were returned home to die with their families. Among them was Geronimo's son Chappo, who was married and had two children of his own. In spite of these deaths by disease, the post doctor seemed to believe that the problem was in the "excessive atmospheric moisture" of the coastal climate. He added in his reports that many of the fatalities were caused by "anxiety and alarm among the Indians" and that they suffered from "mental depression" because they believed the government would not improve their conditions.

Over the next few years several efforts were made to find the Mount Vernon Apaches a new home where they might be more healthy. Geronimo never stopped asking to be returned to their homeland in the Southwest, but as the citizens of that region hated the Apaches, it was decided that it would be unwise to send them back. Land in North Carolina was considered, as was an area in Pennsylvania, where some of the band might be near their children at Carlisle. But problems were encountered with every area suggested, so the Indians remained at Mount Vernon.

An 1893 photo of Apache leaders at Mount Vernon Barracks, Alabama. From left: Chihuahua, Naiche, Loco, Nana, and Geronimo.

In the spring of 1889, the Mescalero Apaches were allowed to return to a reservation on their homeland. Although he loved his family, Geronimo saw this as an opportunity for his wife Ih-tedda, who was a member of that tribe, to escape the squalor of Mount Vernon. She protested leaving, but when he pointed out that people were dying all around them and that by going she might save her life, she agreed. Later he explained in his memoirs, "So many of our people died that I consented to let one of my wives go to the Mescalero Agency in New Mexico to live. This separation is according to our custom equivalent to what the white people call divorce, and she kept our two small children, which she had a right to." Geronimo would see the children again for a short time before he died.

Finally, in 1893, the War Department repealed the amendment forbidding the Apaches to live in the Southwest, and in 1894, they completed plans to relocate the tribe to Fort Sill, Oklahoma Territory. The leaders of the Comanche and Kiowa tribes had been consulted in the matter, and, feeling sorry for the homeless band, had agreed to allow them to come, as long as they stayed near the military base located on the reservation. The Apaches arrived by train on October 4 with almost nothing, as their few possessions had been destroyed in a fire at the railroad freight shed in New Orleans during a stopover there.

Hundreds of Kiowas and Comanches came to meet the newcomers, who they no longer considered as enemies. However, the tribes could not communicate because they spoke different languages. Several years later, Geronimo would learn to speak the Comanche language and become friends with the Comanche leader Quanah Parker.

The following spring, the men in the group built houses with lumber supplied by the army. They were arranged in small villages, with families staying together as they had done when they lived in their own territories. Each man was given a plot of land on which to grow various crops. Altogether, the Apaches raised 250,000 watermelons and cantaloupes in their first year. They ate what they wanted and sold the rest at the post, with the help of the reservation agent's nine-year-old daughter, who stood with them at their wagons and taught them to bargain prices and make change. At first, all the men, including Geronimo, who was by this time over 70, were also required to do other kinds of work. Geronimo and Naiche both became cowhands for the army.

When Geronimo arrived at Fort Sill, the local papers were full of stories calling him a bloodthirsty savage and stating that when he was "captured" he was wearing a blanket made of 99 white scalps taken on his last rampage in the Southwest. (This was a complete fabrication.)

Geronimo and his remaining family members in their melon patch at Fort Sill in the mid-1890s. At left is his wife Zi-yeh; next to Geronimo is his daughter Eva; his son Fenton; and probably his granddaughter Nina Dahkeya.

Because of these reports, the non-Indians who later met Geronimo were often surprised at what they found. One of these was an artist named Eldrige Ayer Burbank who was sent by the Field Museum in Chicago to paint a portrait of the Apache warrior.

When he located Geronimo's house, he was met by "an elderly Indian . . . short, but well built and muscular. His keen, shrewd face was deeply furrowed with strong lines. His small black eyes were watery, but in them there burned a fierce light." He greeted the old man as "Chief Geronimo," which he learned later was much appreciated; the soldiers at the post had nicknamed him Gerry, which he hated. Geronimo called his young daughter Eva to act as interpreter, and asked Burbank many questions about Chicago. Then Geronimo invited Burbank to come inside. He went to an old trunk and pulled out a photograph of himself, handed it to the visitor, and said, "One dollar." Burbank gave him the money, and then used the photograph to explain that he wanted to paint Geronimo's portrait. Geronimo consented, and the two agreed on a price: five dollars for two paintings.

Burbank said that Geronimo was a good model, although, probably out of habit, at the least sound, he would rush to the door and look outside. Twice, Burbank joined Geronimo, his wife Zi-yeh, and Eva for dinner. He said that the food was "excellent." Zi-yeh was in poor health, however, so Geronimo did all the housework, washing the dishes, sweeping the floor, keeping the place immaculate. One day Burbank forgot to wipe his feet at the door and was given a sour look as Geronimo took a broom and swept up the dirt.

Having spent this time with Geronimo, Burbank said that it was hard to imagine him as "leader of a band of ravaging savages." He observed that Geronimo never left the house without putting out a saucer of milk for his cat, and that he loved Eva deeply. "Nobody could be kinder to a child than he was to her," he said. With the money he earned from working and selling souvenirs, Geronimo bought her anything she wanted. And when it was time for her womanhood ceremony, he made it a huge celebration, inviting all the Apaches, and many of the Comanches and Kiowas too.

Burbank also spent time with the other Apaches, including Naiche, who took an interest in painting and often came to watch Burbank work, sometimes for an entire day. Burbank explained his techniques to Naiche, and later sent him a full set of paints from Chicago. When he returned to visit, Naiche presented him with a piece of painted deerskin. Burbank put the deerskin in the Field Museum, and though he met many Indian artists in his lifetime, he later said that Naiche was "by far the best."

A few years later, Geronimo met another white man who would one day record the details of his life: S. M. Barrett, superintendent of the Lawton School, which some of the reservation children had attended for years. When he found out that Barrett had once been wounded by a Mexican, Geronimo became very friendly, and the two began to spend quite a bit of time together. In 1905, Barrett asked Geronimo if he could publish the story of his life. Geronimo agreed, and they settled on payment.

Barrett applied for permission from the army officer in charge, but he said no, adding that, in his opinion, Geronimo should be hanged, not spoiled with so much attention from civilians. Barrett then wrote directly to President Theodore Roosevelt. It took six weeks of writing letters and waiting, but eventually the president gave his permission to proceed, stipulating that the manuscript must be read by the army chief of staff before publication.

It was decided that Daklugie, now called Asa Daklugie, would act as interpreter. The arrangement worked well.

Lenna, one of Geronimo's daughters, photographed probably in 1904. She was described as a "slender, pretty girl with [a] refined and quiet manner."

Asa Daklugie had returned from Carlisle in 1895, fully fluent in English, but still deeply loyal to Geronimo and committed to Apache traditions. He had married a woman named Ramona Chihuahua, daughter of the warrior Chihuahua, who was with Geronimo during his last months as an outlaw. The couple lived with their three children on the reservation.

The three men began in October, sometimes working at Asa Daklugie's house, sometimes at Geronimo's, and sometimes seated outside under the vast prairie sky. At first Geronimo would not allow Barrett to ask questions, saying simply, "Write what I have spoken." But later he agreed to come to Barrett's study and make any corrections he deemed necessary. When the manuscript was finished, it was sent to the army chief of staff, who stated that it was mostly false, and then to Roosevelt, who said it was "very interesting." The president agreed that with a few minor changes the book could be published.

Though his life at Fort Sill consisted mostly of quiet family matters and work, Geronimo was considered a celebrity in his old age. On several occasions he was invited to be an exhibition at fairs and celebrations, and he usually agreed, as long as he was well paid. The first was the Trans-Mississippi and International Exposition, held in Omaha, Nebraska. Naiche and his family went too, but Geronimo was the main attraction. Under guard, they took the train to the fair, and at each station crowds of people came to see the "Apache terror." Geronimo sold the people the buttons off his coat for 25 cents each. Then, between stations, he carefully sewed on new ones from a supply he had brought with him.

On one occasion, Geronimo had his own booth at the Louisiana Purchase Exposition in St. Louis. He spent the day making bows and arrows and selling them, along with autographed photographs, to the tourists. The manager of the fair later admitted to one of the customers,

Geronimo dictating his memoirs to S. M. Barrett (at left). Asa Daklugie (right) acts as interpreter. The book is titled Geronimo's Story of His Life.

"The old gentleman is pretty high priced, but then, he is the only Geronimo."

While in St. Louis, Geronimo got to spend time with his daughter Lenna, whom he had not seen since she and her mother left Mount Vernon. Under supervision, the two were allowed to visit the other shows on the fairgrounds. Geronimo saw "mysterious little brown people" from the Philippines; a magic show in which a woman was seemingly cut into pieces and then reassembled (he believed this worked because of the magician's Power); and a trained bear that was "as intelligent as a man." He also took a ride on the Ferris wheel. Afterward, he said, "I am glad I went to the Fair. I saw many interesting things and learned much of the white people. . . . I wish all my people could have attended the Fair."

The next year he was taken to ride in Theodore Roosevelt's inaugural parade along with other tribal leaders. Geronimo took the opportunity to appeal to the president to return his people to Arizona Territory. He made a long speech ending with, "Great Father, my hands are tied as with a rope. My heart is no longer bad. I will tell my people to obey no chief but the Great White Chief. I pray you to cut the ropes and make me free. Let me die in my own country, an old man who has been punished enough." The president answered, "I have no anger in my heart against you." Then he went on to say that he wished he could let him return, but because the citizens of Arizona Territory still hated him, it was better to stay where he was.

Back on the reservation, many of the Indians had converted to Christianity. At first Geronimo said that this was good for the children, but "I, Geronimo, and these others are too old to travel your Jesus road." Later, however, he felt left out, and began to attend church with the others. Eventually he was baptized in the non-Indians' religion, but, he said, "I have always prayed, and I believe the Almighty has always protected me." In this way, Geronimo did not give up his native religious beliefs, but merely combined them with what he could accept from Christianity. He continued to rely on his own Power, and even treated patients who came to him for healing.

Geronimo outlived most of his friends and family. His son Fenton had died within the first five years at Fort Sill, and Zi-yeh, his young wife, had died in 1904. Then he had only Eva, who was also unwell, and his grandson Thomas. He had many hopes for Thomas, who he felt was "a good student and worker," but in March 1908, he too fell ill and died, at the age of 18. It was a devastating blow for Geronimo, and afterward he began to weaken and became increasingly absentminded. One of the Apaches, who was a child at the time, remembered watching him hunting around for his hat, when all the time it was on his head. When he realized what he had

Geronimo making bows and arrows, which he sold at the Louisiana Purchase Exposition in St. Louis in 1904. In his later years, the Apache leader showed unusual business savvy.

done, Geronimo said with an embarrassed smile, "Why I'm nothing but an old fool."

One cold day in February 1909, Geronimo rode to Lawton to sell some bows and arrows. While he was there, he asked a soldier to buy him some whiskey and then got drunk. On the way home that night, he fell off his horse and landed in a half-frozen puddle. He lay there all night, and a woman found him sometime the next day. He had caught a bad cold, which soon became pneumonia.

Geronimo's family and friends cared for him at home for three days, but when he did not recover, one of his people called for an ambulance to take him to the hospital. Some of the Apaches opposed this move. So many of their people had died at the hospital that they called it the "death house" and tried never to go there. But the doctors insisted that Geronimo be admitted.

At the hospital, Geronimo asked that his surviving children—Eva and Robert—be brought to him, but they were not on the reservation at the time. The officer in charge summoned them by letter instead of by wire, so they arrived too late. On February 17, 1909, at the age of approximately 85, Geronimo died, with Asa Daklugie sitting beside him.

For many years after Geronimo's death, the non-Indian world continued to view him as a vicious, ruthless murderer. Hundreds of paperback wild West adventure novels were written with Geronimo as the villain. Pioneer parents made him into a monster to scare their children, saying, "If you don't behave, Geronimo will get you!" Even as late as 1938, historians such as Frank C. Lockwood, a professor and scholar, wrote that Geronimo was a "cruel, perfidious rascal, hated and distrusted by Apaches and white men alike."

But as the years passed, many Americans began to regard the behavior of the Indians in a new way. When the last of their land had been taken from them and when they had been forced onto reservations where their numbers grew steadily smaller, it became clear that they were victims of a more powerful cruelty than anything Geronimo had been capable of. In light of this changing attitude, Geronimo's skill and determination in resisting the white settlers' invasion of his homeland made him a hero, a symbol of the Indians' relentless efforts to save their land and their way of life, and, for some, a symbol of the universal fight for freedom and justice.

CHRONOLOGY

ca. 1823   Born near the Gila River in present-day Arizona

1838   Father dies; takes over support of mother

1841   Accepted into Nednai council of warriors; marries Alope

1850   Mother, Alope, and three children killed by Mexicans at Janos

1851   Directs Apache attack at Arizpe, Mexico, to avenge Janos massacre; marries Chee-hash-kish, mother of Chappo and Dohn-say; marries Nana-tha-thtith

1855   Nana-tha-thtith and child killed by Mexicans

1858   Goes to live with Chiricahua Apaches under Cochise

1861   Cut the Tent Affair begins Apache-American wars

1872   General Howard negotiates treaty with Cochise; Geronimo lives peacefully on Chiricahua reservation

1876   Escapes Agent Clum to avoid going to San Carlos

1877   Arrested at Warm Springs reservation; taken to San Carlos reservation

1878   Breaks out; goes to Mexico

1880   Surrenders to General Willcox at San Bernardino; returns to San Carlos

1881   Breaks out; meets up with other "outlaw" bands in Sierra Madre

1883   Surrenders at mountain hideout to General Crook

1885   Breaks out of San Carlos for the last time

March 1886   Surrenders to General Crook at Cañón de los Embudos, then breaks away again

Aug. 1886   Surrenders to General Miles

Oct. 1886   Transported to Fort Pickens, Florida, as prisoner of war

1888   Transferred to Mount Vernon Barracks, Alabama

1894   Moved to reservation at Fort Sill, Oklahoma

1905   Rides in President Theodore Roosevelt's inaugural parade

Feb. 17, 1909   Dies at Fort Sill reservation

FURTHER READING

Adams, Alexander. *Geronimo*. New York: Putnam, 1971.

Ball, Eve. *In the Days of Victorio: Recollections of a Warm Springs Apache*. Tucson: University of Arizona Press, 1970.

Barrett, S. M. *Geronimo's Story of His Life*. 1906. New York: Ballantine Books, 1978.

Betinez, Jason. *I Fought with Geronimo*. Harrisburg, PA: Stackpole, 1959.

Carter, Forrest. *Watch for Me on the Mountain: A Novel of Geronimo and the Apache Nation*. New York: Delacorte Press, 1978.

Clum, Woodworth. *Apache Agent: The Story of John P. Clum*. Boston: Houghton Mifflin, 1936.

Cremony, John Carey. *Life Among the Apaches*. 1868. Glorieta, NM: Rio Grande Press, 1969.

Davis, Britton. *The Truth About Geronimo*. New Haven: Yale University Press, 1929.

Debo, Angie. *Geronimo: The Man, His Time, His Place*. Norman: University of Oklahoma Press, 1976.

Faulk, Odie B. *The Geronimo Campaign*. New York: Oxford University Press, 1969.

Howard, Oliver Otis. *My Life and Experiences Among Our Hostile Indians*. New York: Da Capo Press, 1972.

Sonnichsen, C. L., ed. *Geronimo and the End of the Apache Wars*. Lincoln: University of Nebraska Press, 1990.

INDEX

PICTURE CREDITS

MELISSA SCHWARZ is a freelance writer and book editor with a longtime interest in the American Western frontier. She is the author of *Cochise*, another biography in the Chelsea House series NORTH AMERICAN INDIANS OF ACHIEVEMENT. Ms. Schwarz currently lives in New York City.

W. DAVID BAIRD is the Howard A. White Professor of History at Pepperdine University in Malibu, California. He holds a Ph.D. from the University of Oklahoma and was formerly on the faculty of history at the University of Arkansas, Fayetteville, and Oklahoma State University. He has served as president of both the Western History Association, a professional organization, and Phi Alpha Theta, the international honor society for students of history. Dr. Baird is also the author of *The Quapaw Indians: A History of the Downstream People* and *Peter Pitchlynn: Chief of the Choctaws* and the editor of *A Creek Warrior of the Confederacy: The Autobiography of Chief G. W. Grayson.*